Emily Sarah Holt

The Gold That Glitters

Emily Sarah Holt

The Gold That Glitters

ISBN/EAN: 9783743312777

Manufactured in Europe, USA, Canada, Australia, Japa

Cover: Foto ©ninafisch / pixelio.de

Manufactured and distributed by brebook publishing software (www.brebook.com)

Emily Sarah Holt

The Gold That Glitters

The
Gold that Glitters;

OR,

THE MISTAKES OF JENNY LAVENDER.

BY

EMILY SARAH HOLT,

AUTHOR OF
"MISTRESS MARGERY;" "SISTER ROSE;" "AT THE GRENE GRIFFIN;"
ETC.

NEW EDITION.

JOHN F. SHAW AND CO., LTD.,
Publishers,
3, PILGRIM STREET, LONDON, E.C.

CONTENTS.

CHAPTER I.
JENNY PREPARES TO GO A-JOURNEYING

CHAPTER II.
HOW JENNY FARED THE FIRST EVENING.

CHAPTER III.
THE GOLD THAT GLITTERS

CHAPTER IV.
SUDDEN CHANGES

CHAPTER V.
WILL JACKSON REAPPEARS

CHAPTER VI.
WHEREIN JENNY MAKES HER LAST MISTAKE

"She watched the sun sinking slowly to the west."

THE GOLD THAT GLITTERS.

CHAPTER I.

JENNY PREPARES TO GO A-JOURNEYING.

"JENNY, my dear maid, thou wilt never fetch white meal out of a sack of sea-coal."

Jenny tossed her head. It would have been a nice little brown head, if it had not been quite so fond of tossing itself. But Jenny was just sixteen, and laboured under a delusion which besets young folks of that age — namely, that half the brains in the world had got into her head, and very few had been left in her grandmother's.

"I don't know what you mean, Grandmother," said Jenny, as an accompaniment to that toss.

"O Jenny, Jenny! what a shocking thing of you to say, when you knew what your grandmother meant as well as you knew your name was Jane Lavender!"

"I rather think thou dost, my lass," said old Mrs. Lavender quietly.

"Well, I suppose you mean to run down Mr. Featherstone," said Jenny, pouting. "You're always running him down. And there isn't a bit of use in it—not with me. I like him, and I always shall. He's such a gentleman, and always so soft-spoken. But I believe you like that clod-hopper Tom Fenton, ever so much better. I can't abide him."

"There's a deal more of the feather than the stone about Robin Featherstone, lass. If he be a stone, he's a rolling one. Hasn't he been in three places since he came here?"

"Yes, because they didn't use him right in none of 'em. Wanted him to do things out of his place, and such like. Why, at Hampstead Hall, they set him to chop wood."

"Well, why not?" asked Mrs. Lavender, knitting away.

"Because it wasn't his place," answered Jenny, indignantly. "It made his hands all rough, and he's that like a gentleman he couldn't stand it."

"Tom Fenton would have done it, I shouldn't wonder."

"As if it would have mattered to Tom Fenton, with his great red hands! They couldn't be no rougher than they are, if he chopped wood while Christmas. Besides, it's his trade—wood-chopping is. Mr. Featherstone's some'at better nor a carpenter."

"They're honest hands, if they are red, Jenny."

"And he's a cast in his eyes."

"Scarcely. Anyhow, he's none in his heart."

"And his nose turns up!"

"Not as much as thine, Jenny."

"Mine!" cried Jenny, in angry amazement. "Grandmother, what will you say next? My nose is as straight as—as the church tower."

"Maybe it is, in general, my lass. But just now thou art turning it up at poor Tom."

"'Poor Tom,' indeed!" said Jenny, in a disgusted tone. "He'd best not come after me, or I'll 'poor Tom' him. I want none of him, I can tell you."

"Well, Jenny, don't lose thy temper over Tom, or Robin either. Thou 'rt like the most of maids—they'll never heed the experience of old folks. If thou wilt not be 'ruled by the rudder, thou must be ruled by the rock.' 'All is not gold that glitters,' and I'm afeard thou shalt find it so, poor soul! But I can't put wisdom into thee; I can only pray the Lord to give it thee. Be thy bags packed up?"

"Ay," said Jenny, rather sulkily.

"And all ready to set forth?"

"There's just a few little things to see to yet."

"Best go and see to them, then."

Mrs. Lavender knitted quietly on, and Jenny shut the door with a little more of a slam than it quite needed, and ran up to her own room, where she slept with her elder sister.

"Jenny, thy bags are not locked," said her sister, as she came in.

"Oh, let be, Kate, do! Grandmother's been at me with a whole heap of her old saws, till I'm worn out. I wish nobody had ever spoke one of 'em."

"What's the matter?"

"Oh, she's at me about Robin Featherstone: wants me to give up keeping company with him, and all that. Tom Fenton's her pattern man, and a pretty pattern he is. I wouldn't look at him if there wasn't another man in Staffordshire. Robin's a gentleman, and Tom's a clown."

"I don't see how you are to give up Robin, when you are going into the very house where he lives."

"Of course not. 'Tis all rubbish! I wish old women would hold their tongues. I'm not going to Bentley Hall to sit mewed up in my mistress' chamber, turning up the whites of my eyes, and singing Psalms through my nose. I mean to lead a jolly life there, I can tell you, for all Grandmother. It really is too bad of old folks, that can't knock about and enjoy their lives, to pen up young maids like so many sheep. I shall never be young but once, and I want some pleasure in my life."

"All right," said Kate lightly. "I scarce think they turn up the whites of their eyes at Bentley Hall. Have your fling, Jenny—only don't go *too* far, look you."

"I can take care of myself, thank you," returned Jenny scornfully. "Lock that striped bag for me, Kate, there's a darling; there's father calling downstairs."

And Jenny ran off, to cry softly in a high treble to Kate, a minute afterwards—"Supper!"

Supper was spread in the large kitchen of the farmhouse. Jenny's father was a tenant farmer, his landlord being Colonel Lane, of Bentley Hall, and it was to be maid (or, as they said then, "lady's woman") to the Colonel's sister, that Jenny was going to the Hall. Mrs. Jane was much younger than her brother, being only six years older than Jenny herself. In the present day she would be called Miss Jane, but in 1651 only little girls were termed *Miss*. Jenny had always been rather a pet, both with Mrs. Lane and her daughter; for she was a bright child, who learned easily, and could repeat the Creed and the Ten Commandments as glibly as possible when she was only six years old. Unhappily, lessons were apt to run out of Jenny's head as fast as they ran in, except when frequently demanded; but the Creed and the Commandments had to stay there, for every Saturday night she was called on to repeat them to her Grandmother, and every Sunday afternoon she had to say them at the catechising in church. In Jenny's head, therefore, they remained; but down to Jenny's heart they never penetrated.

It was only now that Mrs. Jane was setting up a maid for herself. Hitherto she had been served by her mother's woman; but now she was going on a visit to some relatives near

Bristol, and it was thought proper that she should have a woman of her own. And when the question was asked where the maid should be sought, Mrs. Jane had said at once — "Oh, let me have little Jenny Lavender!"

Farmer Lavender was not quite so ready to let Jenny go as Mrs. Jane was to ask it. Bristol seemed to him a long way off, and, being a town, most likely a wicked place. Those were days in which people made their wills before they took a journey of a hundred miles; and no wonder, when the roads were so bad that men had frequently to be hired to walk beside a gentleman's carriage, and give it a push to either side, when it showed an inclination to topple over; or oxen sometimes were fetched, to pull the coach out of a deep quagmire of mud, from which only one half of it was visible. So Farmer Lavender shook his head, and said "he didn't know, no, he didn't, whether he'd let his little maid go." But Mrs. Jane was determined—and so was

Jenny; and between them they conquered the farmer, though his old mother was on the prudent side. This was Friday, and Mrs. Jane was to leave home on Tuesday; and on Saturday afternoon, Robert Featherstone, Colonel Lane's valet, whom Jenny thought such a gentleman, was to come for her and her luggage.

If a gentleman be a man who never does any useful thing that he can help, then Mr. Robin Featherstone was a perfect gentleman—much more so than his master, who was ready to put his hand to any work that wanted doing. Mr. Featherstone thought far more of his elegant white hands than the Colonel did of his, and oiled his chestnut locks at least three times as often. He liked the Colonel's service, because he had very little to do, and there were plenty of people in the house as idle and feather-pated as himself. Colonel Lane was in Robin's eyes a good master, though old Mrs. Lavender thought him a bad one. That is, he allowed his servants to neglect their work with very little censure, and took no notice of their employments during their leisure hours. And Satan was not a bit less busy in 1651 than he is in 1895, in finding mischief for idle hands to do. Leisure time is to a man what he chooses to make it—either a great blessing or a great curse. And just then, for those who chose the last, the disturbed and unsettled state of the country offered particular opportunities.

The war between the King and the Parliament was just over. Charles the First had been beheaded at Whitehall nearly two years before; and though his son, Charles II., was still in England, fighting to recover his father's kingdom, it was pretty plainly to be seen that his struggle was a hopeless one. The great battle of Worcester, which ended the long conflict, had been fought about three weeks before, and the young King had only just escaped with his life, through the bravery of his gallant troops, who made a desperate stand in the street, keeping the victors at bay while their commander fled to a place of concealment.

The Cavaliers, as Charles's troops were called, had few virtues beyond their loyalty and courage. After their dispersion at Worcester, they spread over the country in small parties, begging, stealing, or committing open ravages. Many of the Parliamentary troops —not all—were grave, sensible, God-fearing men, who were only concerned to do what they believed was right and righteous. Much fewer of the Cavaliers had any such aim, beyond their devotion to the monarchy, and their enthusiastic determination to uphold it. They were mostly gay, rollicking fellows, with little principle, and less steadfastness, who squandered their money on folly, if nothing worse; and then helped themselves to other people's goods without any uneasiness of conscience.

Colonel Lane was a Cavalier, and devoted to the King, and most of his tenants were Cavaliers also. A few were Roundheads— staunch adherents of the Parliament; and a few more had no very strong convictions on either side, and while they chiefly preferred the monarchy, would have been content with any settlement which allowed them to live honest and peaceable lives. Old Mrs. Lavender belonged to this last class. If asked which side she was on, she would have said, "For the King"; but in her heart she had no enmity to either. Her son was a warmer politician; Jenny, being sixteen, was a much warmer still, and as Robin Featherstone, her hero, was a Cavalier, so of course was she.

We have given the worthy farmer and his family a good while to sit down to supper, which that night included a kettle of furmety, a mermaid pie, and a taffaty tart. What were they? A very reasonable question, especially as to the mermaid pie, since mermaids are rather scarce articles in the market. Well, a mermaid pie was made of pork and eels, and was terribly rich and indigestible; a taffaty tart was an apple-pie, seasoned with lemon-peel and fennel-seed; and the receipt for furmety—a very famous and favourite dish with our forefathers—I give as it stands in a curious little book, entitled, *The Compleat Cook*, printed in 1683.

"Take a quart of cream, a quarter of a pound of French barley, the whitest you can get, and boyl it very tender in three or four several waters, and let it be cold; then put both together. Put into it a blade of mace, a nutmeg cut in quarters, a race of ginger cut in four or five pieces, and so let it boyl a good while, still stirring, and season it with sugar to your taste; then take the yolks of four eggs, and beat them with a little cream, and stir them into it, and so let it boyl a little after the eggs are in: then have ready blanched and beaten twenty almonds (kept from oyling), with a little rose-water; then take a boulter strainer, and rub your almonds with a little of your furmity through the strainer, but set on the fire no more: and stir in a little salt, and a little sliced nutmeg, pickt out of the great pieces of it, and put it in a dish, and serve it."

The farmhouse family consisted only of Farmer Lavender, his mother, and his two daughters, Kate and Jenny. But fifteen people sat down to supper: for the whole household, including the farmer's men down to the little lad who scared the crows, all ate together in the big kitchen. Mrs. Lavender sat at the head of the table, the farmer at the other end, with Jenny on his right hand: for there was in the father's heart a very warm place for his motherless Jenny.

"All ready to set forth, my lass?" he said gently—perhaps a little sadly.

"Yes, Father, all ready."

"Art thou glad to go, child?"

"I'd like well to see the world, Father."

"Well, well! I mind the time when I'd ha' been pleased enough to have thy chance, my lass. Be a good girl, and forget not the good ways thy grandmother has learned thee, and then I cast no doubt thou'lt do well."

Jenny assented with apparent meekness, inwardly purposing to forget them as fast as she could. She ran into the garden when supper was over, to gather a nosegay, if possible, of the few flowers left at that time of year. She was just tucking a bit of southernwood into her bodice, when a voice on the other side of the hedge said softly,—

"Jenny."

"Well, what do you want, Tom Fenton?" responded Jenny, in a tone which was not calculated to make her visitor feel particularly welcome.

It was one of Jenny's standing grievances against Tom, that he would call her by her name. Robin Featherstone called her plain "Mrs. Jenny," which pleased her vanity much better.

"You're really going to-morrow, Jenny?"

"Of course I am," said Jenny.

"You'll forget me, like as not," said Tom, earnestly hoping to be contradicted.

"Of course I shall," replied Jenny flippantly.

"I wish you wouldn't, Jenny," said Tom, with a meek humility that should have disarmed Jenny's resentment, but only increased it. Like many other foolish people, Jenny was apt to mistake pert speeches for cleverness, and gentleness for want of manly spirit.

"I wish you wouldn't, Jenny. There isn't a soul as thinks as much of you as I do, not in all the country-side. Nor there isn't one as 'll miss you like me."

"I just wish you 'd take up with somebody else, and give over plaguing me," said Jenny mercilessly. "There's Ruth Merston, and Dolly Campion, and Abigail——"

"I don't want ne'er a one on 'em," answered Tom, in a rather hurt tone. "I've never thought, not a minute, o' nobody but you, Jenny, not since we was a little lad and lass together. I've always loved you, Jenny. Haven't you ne'er a kind word for me afore we part? May be a long day ere we shall meet again."

"I'm sure I hope it will," said Jenny, half vexed at Tom's pertinacity, and half amusing herself, for she thought it good fun to tease him.

"Don't you care the least bit for me, Jenny, dear?"

"No, I don't. Why should I?"

"But you used, Jenny, once. Didn't you, now? That day I brought you them blue ribbons you liked so well, you said—don't you mind what you said, dear heart?"

"I said a deal o' nonsense, I shouldn't wonder. Don't be a goose, Tom! You can't think to bind a girl to what she says when you give her blue ribbons."

"I'd be bound to what I said, ribbons or no ribbons," said Tom firmly. "But I see how it is—it's that scented idiot, Featherstone, has come betwixt you and me. O Jenny, my dear love, don't you listen to him! He'll not be bound to a word he says the minute it's not comfortable to keep it. He'll just win your heart, Jenny, and then throw you o' one side like a withered flower, as soon as ever he sees a fresh one as suits him better. My dear maid—"

"I'm sure I'm mighty obliged to you, Mr. Fenton!" said Jenny, really angry now. "It's right handsome of you to liken me to a withered flower. Mr. Featherstone's a gentleman in a many ot his ways, and that's more nor you are, and I wish you good evening.'

"Jenny, my dear, don't 'ee, now ——"

But Jenny was gone.

Tom turned sorrowfully away. Before he had taken two steps, he was arrested by a kindly voice.

"You made a mistake, there, Tom," it said. "But don't you lose heart; it isn't too bad to be got over."

Tom stopped at once, and went back to the hedge, whence that kindly voice had spoken.

"Is that you, Kate?" he said.

"Ay," answered the voice of Jenny's sister. Kate was not a very wise girl, but she was less flighty and foolish than Jenny; and she had a kind heart, which made her always wish to help anyone in trouble. "Tom, don't be in a taking; but you've made a mistake, as I said. You know not how to handle such a maid as Jenny."

"What should I have said, Kate? I'm fair beat out of heart, and you'll make me out of charity with myself if you tell me 't is my own fault."

"Oh, not so ill as that, Tom! But next time she bids you go and take up with somebody else, just tell her you mean to do so, and 'there are as good fish in the sea as ever came out of it.' That's the way to tackle the likes of her; not to look struck into the dumps, and fetch sighs like a windmill."

"But I don't mean it, Kate," said Tom, looking puzzled.

"Oh, be not so peevish, Tom! Can't you *say* so?"

"No," answered Tom, with sudden gravity; "I can't, truly. I've alway looked for Jenny to be my wife one day, ever since I was as high as those palings; but I'll not win her by untruth. There'd be no blessing from the Lord on that sort of work. I can't, Kate Lavender."

"Well, I never did hear the like!" exclaimed Kate. "You can't think so much of Jenny as I reckoned you did, if you stick at nought in that way."

"I think more of Jenny than of anyone else in the world, Kate, and you know it," said Tom, with a dignity which Kate could not help feeling. "But I think more yet of Him that's above the world. No, no! If ever I win Jenny—and God grant I may! —I'll win her righteously, not lyingly. I thank you for your good meaning, all the same."

"Good even to you both!" said an old man's voice; and they turned to see the speaker coming down the lane. He was a venerable-looking man, clad in a long brown coat, girt to him by a band of rough leather; his long, silvery hair fell over his shoulders, and under his arm was a large, clasped book, in a leather cover which had seen much service.

"Uncle Anthony!" cried Tom. "I knew not you were back. Are you on your way up the hill? Here, prithee, leave me carry your book. Good even, Kate, and I thank you!"

"Good even!" said Kate, with a nod to both; and Tom tucked the big book under his own arm, and went forward with the traveller.

CHAPTER II.

How Jenny Fared the First Evening.

CHAPTER II.

HOW JENNY FARED THE FIRST EVENING.

"WELL, for sure, Aunt Persis will be some fain to see you!" said Tom Fenton, as he and his uncle, old Anthony, went forward up the hill. "But whence come you, now, Uncle? Are you very weary? Eh, but I'm glad you've won home safe!"

"God bless thee, my lad! Ay, He's brought me home safe. A bit footsore, to be sure, and glad enough of rest: but gladder to be suffered to do His will, and minister to His suffering servants. Whence come I? Well, from Kidderminster, to-day; but——"

"Dear heart! but you never footed it all the way from Kidderminster?"

"No, no, dear lad. A good man gave me a lift for a matter o' eight miles or more. But, dear me! I mind the time I could ha' run nigh on a mile in five minutes, and ha' trudged my forty mile a day, nor scarce felt it. I reckon, Tom, lad, thou 'rt not so lissome as I was at thy years. Well, to be sure! 'Tis all right; I'm only a good way nearer Home."

They walked on together for a few minutes in silence. Tom's thoughts had gone back from the momentary pleasure of welcoming his uncle, to whom he was greatly attached, to his sore disappointment about Jenny.

"What is it, Tom?" said the old man quietly.

"Oh, only a bit of trouble, Uncle. Nought I need cumber you with."

"Jenny Lavender?" was the next suggestion.

"Ay. I thought not you knew how I'd set my heart on her, ever since she was that high," said Tom, indicating a length of about a yard. "I've never thought o' none but her all my life. But she's that taken up with a sorry popinjay of a fellow, she'll not hear me now. I'd always thought Jenny'd be my wife."

Poor Tom's voice was very doleful, for his heart was sore.

"Thou'd alway thought so," said the quiet voice. "But what if the Lord thinks otherway, Tom?"

Tom came to a sudden stop.

"Uncle Anthony! Eh, but you don't——" and Tom's words went no further.

"My lad, thou'rt but a babe in Christ. 'T isn't so many months since thou first set foot in the narrow way. Dost thou think He means Jenny Lavender for thee, and that thy feet should run faster in the way of His commandments for having her running alongside thee? Art thou well assured she wouldn't run the other way?"

Old Anthony had spoken the truth. Tom was but a very young Christian, of some six months' standing. He had never dreamed of any antagonism arising between his love to Christ and his love to Jenny Lavender. Stay—had he not? What was that faint something, without a name— a sort of vague uneasiness, which had seemed to creep over him whenever he had seen her during those months—a sense of incongruity between her light prattle and his own inmost thoughts and holiest feelings? It was so slight that as yet he had never faced it. He recognised now it was because his heart had refused to face it. And conscience told him, speaking loudly this time, that he must hold back no longer.

"Uncle Anthony," he said, in a troubled voice, "I'm sore afeard I've not set the Lord afore me in that matter. I never saw it so afore. But now you've set me on it, I can't deny that we shouldn't pull same way. But what then? Must I give her up? Mayn't I pray the Lord to touch her heart, and give her to me, any longer?"

The old man looked into the sorrowful

eyes of the young man, whom he loved as dearly as if he had been his own son.

"Dear lad," he said, "pray the Lord to bring her to Himself. That's safe to be His will, for He willeth not the death of a sinner. But as to giving her to thee, if I were thou, Tom, I'd leave that with Him. Meantime, thy way's plain. 'Be ye not unequally yoked together.' The command's clear as daylight. Never get a clog to thy soul. Thou canst live without Jenny Lavender; but couldst thou live without Jesus Christ?"

Tom shook his head, without speaking.

"To tell truth, Tom, I'm not sorry she's going away. Maybe the Lord's sending her hence, either to open her eyes and send her back weary and cloyed with the world she's going into so gaily now, or else to open thine, and show thee plain, stripped of outside glitter, the real thing she is, that thou mayest see what a sorry wife she would make to a Christian man. No, I'm not sorry. And unless I mistake greatly, Tom, the time's coming when thou shalt not be sorry neither. In the meantime, 'tarry thou the Lord's leisure.' If He be the chief object of thy desire, thy desire is safe to be fulfilled. 'This is the will of God, even our sanctification.'"

They turned to the left at the top of the hill, and went a few yards along the lane, to a little cottage embowered in ivy, which was Anthony's home.

"Wilt thou come in, Tom, lad?"

"No, Uncle, I thank you. You've opened my eyes, but it's made 'em smart a bit too much to face the light as yet. I'll take a sharp trudge over the moor, and battle it out with myself."

"Take the Lord with thee, lad. Satan'll have thee down if thou doesn't. He's strong and full o' wiles, and if he can't conquer thee in his black robe, he'll put on a white one. There's no harm in thy saying to the Lord, 'Lord, Thou knowest that I love Jenny Lavender'; but take care that it does not come before, 'Lord, Thou knowest that I love *Thee.*' Maybe He's putting the same question to thee to-night, that He did to Peter at the lake-side."

"Ay, ay, Uncle. I'll not forget. God bless thee!"

Tom wrung old Anthony's hand, and turned away.

One moment the old man paused before he went in.

"Lord, Thou lovest the lad better than I do," he said, half aloud. "Do Thy best for him!"

Then he lifted the latch, and met a warm welcome from his wife Persis.

* * * * * *

"Mrs. Jenny, your servant!" said the smooth tones of Robin Featherstone at the farmhouse door, about twenty hours later. "The horse awaits your good pleasure, and will only be less proud to bear you than I shall to ride before you."

Jenny's silly little heart fluttered at the absurd compliment.

"Farewell, Grandmother," she said, going up to the old lady. "Pray, your blessing."

Old Mrs. Lavender laid her trembling hand on the girl's head.

"May God bless thee, my maid, and make thee a blessing! I have but one word for thee at the parting, and if thou wilt take it as thy motto for life, thou mayest do well. 'Look to the end.' Try the ground afore thou settest down thy foot. 'Many a cloudy morrow turneth out a fair day,' and ''Tis ill to get in the hundred and lose in the shire.' So look to the end, Jenny, and be wise in time. 'All that glittereth is not gold,' and all gold does not glitter, specially when folk's eyes be shut. We say down in my country, 'There's a hill against a stack all Craven through,' and thou'lt find it so. God keep thee!"

Jenny's father gave her a warm embrace and a hearty blessing, and his hand went to his eyes as he turned to Robin Featherstone.

"Fare you well, Robin," said he, "and have a care of my girl."

The elegant Mr. Featherstone laid his hand upon that portion of his waiscoat which was supposed to cover his heart.

"Mr. Lavender, it will be the pride of my heart to serve Mrs. Jenny, though it cost my life."

He sprang on the brown horse, and Jenny, helped by her father, mounted the pillion behind him. Women very seldom rode alone at that day.

Kate ran after them, as they started, with an old shoe in her hand, which she delivered with such good (or bad) effect that it hit the horse on the ear, and made it shy. Happily, it was a sedate old quadruped, not given to giddy ways, and quickly recovered itself.

"Good luck!" cried Kate, as they rode away.

A second horse followed, ridden by one of Colonel Lane's stable-boys, carrying Jenny's two bags.

It was not a mile from the farm to Bentley Hall, and they were soon in the stableyard, where Jenny alighted, and was taken by Featherstone into the servants' hall, where with another complimentary flourish he introduced her to the rest of the household.

"My lords and ladies, I have the honour to present to you the Lady Jane Lavender."

"Now you just get out of my way, with your lords and ladies," said the cook, pushing by them. "Good even, Jenny. We've seen Jenny Lavender afore, every man jack of us."

Mr. Featherstone got out of the way without much delay, for the cook had a gridiron in his hand, and he had been known before now to box somebody's ears with that instrument.

He recovered his dignity as soon as he could, and suggested that Jenny should go up to the chamber of her new mistress.

"Maybe Mrs. Millicent should be pleased to take her," he said, making a low bow to Mrs. Lane's maid.

"She knows her way upstairs as well as

I do," answered Millicent bluntly. "Have done with your airs, Robin! and prithee don't put Jenny up to 'em.

"Now, Jenny, you run up and wait for Mrs. Jane; she'll be there in a minute, most like. You can hang your hood and cloak behind the door."

There were no bonnets in those days, nor shawls; women wore hoods or tall hats on their heads when they went out, and cloaks in cold weather; when it was warm they merely tied on a muslin or linen tippet, fastening it with a bow of ribbon at the throat.

The gown sleeves then came down mostly to the wrist; but sometimes only to the elbows, where they were finished with a little frill. How the neck was covered, in the house, depended on its owner's notions. If she were gay and fashionable, it was not covered at all. But if she were sensible and quiet, she generally wore the same kind of muslin tippet that was used on warm days out of doors. Old women sometimes wore the close frill round the neck, which had been used in Queen Elizabeth's time; but this was quite gone out of fashion for younger ones.

Mrs. Jane's room was empty. Jenny knew her way to it well enough, for she had often been there before; but her heart beat high when she saw something in the corner that had never been there before—a neat, little low bed, covered with a quilt of coarse, padded blue silk. That was for Jenny, as Jenny knew. The room was long, low, and somewhat narrow. Four windows, so close together as to have the effect of one, ran along the whole length of one end, filled with small diamond-shaped panes of greenish glass.

In the midst of these stood a toilet-table, whereon were a number of pots and boxes, the uses of which were as yet unknown to the new maid. The large bed was hung with flowered cherry-coloured satin; an inlaid chair, filled with cushions, stood before the fireplace, and a small Turkey carpet lay in front of it.

Jenny stood contemplating everything, with a sense of great elation to think that her place henceforward would be in the midst of all this comfort and grandeur. Suddenly a quick step ran up the polished staircase, the door opened, and a young lady made her made her appearance.

Her description will serve for the ladies of that day in general.

Her skirt came just down to the foot, and was moderately full; it was made of green satin. Over this was the actual gown, of tawny or yellowish-brown silk, trimmed with silver lace. The skirt was open in front, and was bunched up all round so as barely to reach the knees. The bodice, which was tight to the figure, was laced up in front with silver; it was cut low on the neck, and over it was a tippet of clear muslin, tied with green ribbon to match the skirt. The sleeves were slightly fulled, and were finished by very deep cuffs of similar muslin, midway between the wrist and the elbow. The young lady's hair was dressed in a small knob behind; it

P

came a little over the forehead at the front in a point, and flowed down at the sides in slender ringlets.

"Oh, Jenny, are you come? That is right," said she.

"Yes, madam, to serve you," answered Jenny, dropping a courtesy.

"Very good. Here, pick up these pins, and put them into that box. You must learn to dress me, and dress my hair. Dear me, you have all to learn! Well, never mind; the best woman living had to begin once."

"Yes, madam," said smiling Jenny.

Mrs. Jane sat down before the toilet-table, and with more rapidity than Jenny could well follow, showed her the articles upon it, and the uses for which they were designed.

"Here is pearl powder; that is for my forehead. This is rouge, for my cheeks and lips. Now, mind what you do with them! Don't go and put the white powder on my cheeks, and the red upon my nose! This is pomatum for my hair; and this empty box holds my love-locks (you'll have to learn how to put those in, Jenny); in this bottle is a wash for my face. I don't dye my hair, nor use oils for my hands—one must draw the line somewhere. But the other matters you must learn to apply."

Jenny listened in silent amazement. She had never realised till that moment what an artificial flower her young mistress was.

Her own cosmetics were soap and water; and she was divided between disgust and admiration at the number of Mrs. Jane's beautifiers. Poor Jenny had no idea that Mrs. Jane used a very moderate amount of them, as contrasted with most fashionable ladies of her day.

"I must have a word with you, Jenny, as to your manners," said Mrs. Jane, more gravely. "I can't do to have you falling in love with anybody. It would be very inconvenient, and, in fact, there's nobody here for you. Remember *now*, you are above Featherstone and all the men-servants; and you must not set your cap at the chaplain, because he's Mrs. Millicent's property."

Above that elegant gentleman, Mr. Featherstone! Jenny felt as if she trod on perfumed air. She was not in the least surprised to be told that she was not to marry the chaplain; the family chaplain, of whom there was one in every family of any pretension, was considered a poor mean creature, whose natural wife was the lady's maid; and Jenny quite understood that Mrs. Millicent took precedence of her.

"You take your seat at table, Jenny, next below Mrs. Millicent. Of course you know you are not to speak there? If any one should have such ill-manners as to address you, you must answer quite respectfully, but as short as possible. Well, now to tell you your duties. You rise every morning at five of the clock; dress quietly, and when you are ready, wake me, if I have not woke sooner. Then you dress me, go with me to prayers in the chapel, then to breakfast in the hall; in the morning (when I am at home) you follow me about in my duties in the kitchen, still-room, and dairy; you help me to see to the poultry, get up my muslins and laces, and mend my clothes. In the afternoon you go out visiting with me, work tapestry, embroider, or spin. In the evening, if there be music or dancing, you can join; if not, you keep to your needle."

Jenny courtesied, and meekly "hoped she should do her duty." Some portions of this duty, now explained to her, were sufficiently to her taste; others sounded very uninteresting. These were the usual services expected from a lady's maid two hundred years ago.

"Very well," said Mrs. Jane, looking round. "I think that is all at the present. If I think of any other matter, I will mention it. Now ring that little bell on the sidetable, and Millicent shall give you your first lesson in dressing my hair."

Jenny found that first lesson a trial. Millicent was quick and precise; she gave her instructions almost sharply, and made little allowance for Jenny's ignorance and inaptitude.

She seemed to expect her to know what to do without being told, or at the utmost to need only once telling. Jenny found it necessary to have all her wits about her, and began to think that her new situation was not quite so perfect a Paradise as she had supposed it.

From this exercise they went down to supper in the hall, where Jenny found herself placed at the higher table between Millicent and the steward — a stiff, silent, elderly man, who never said a word to her all supper-time. Robin Featherstone sat at the lower table; for the two tables made the only distinction between the family and the household, who all ate together in the hall.

The next discovery was that she must never ask for a second helping, but must take what was given her and be content. Accustomed to the freedom and plenty of the farmhouse kitchen, Jenny sadly felt the constraint of her new life. She was obliged to fall back for her consolation on the pleasure of her elevation above all her old associates. It was rather poor fare.

When, after assisting Mrs. Jane to undress, with sundry snubbings from Millicent, and some not ill-natured laughter from her young mistress at Jenny's blunders, she was at last free to lie down to rest herself, she was conscious of a little doubt, whether the appellation of "Mrs. Jenny," the higher place at the table, and the distinction of being nobody in the drawing-room, were quite as agreeable as plenty to eat and drink, and liberty to run into the garden, dance and sing whenever she chose to do so.

The Sunday which followed was spent as the Holy Day was wont to be spent by Cavalier families who were respectable and not riotous.

The Lanes were members of the Church of England, but the Church had been abolished, so far as it lay in the power of those in authority at that time. Many of the clergy were turned out of their livings—it cannot be denied that some of them had deserved it—and the Book of Common Prayer was stringently suppressed. No man dared to use it now, except secretly. Those solemn and beautiful prayers, offered up by many generations, and endeared to their children as only childhood's memories can endear, might not be uttered, save in fear and trembling, in the dead of night, or in hushed whispers in the day-time.

Early in the morning, before the world was astir, a few of Colonel Lane's family met the chaplain in the private chapel, and there in low voices the morning prayers were read, and the responses breathed. There was no singing nor chanting; that would have been too much to dare. The men who had themselves suffered so much for holding secret conventicles, and preferring one style of prayer to another, now drove their fellow-countrymen into the very same acts, and imposed on them the same sufferings.

This secret service over, the family met at breakfast, after which they drove in the great family coach to Darlaston Church. The present Vicar, if he may so be termed, was an independent minister. These ministers, who alone were now permitted to minister, were of three kinds.

Some were true Christians—often very ripely spiritual ones—who preached Christ, and let politics alone. Another class were virulent controversialists, who preached politics, and too often let Christianity alone. And a third consisted of those concealed Jesuits whom Rome had sent over for the purpose of stirring up dissension, some of whom professed to be clergy of the Church, and some Nonconformists.

The gentleman just now officiating at Darlaston belonged to the second class. His sermon was a violent diatribe against kings in general, and "Charles Stuart" in particular, to which the few Royalists in his congregation had to listen with what patience they might.

Jenny Lavender did not carry away a word of it. Her head was full of the honour and glory of driving in the Bentley Hall coach (wherein she occupied the lowest seat by the door), and of sitting in the Bentley Hall pew.

She only hoped that Ruth Merston and Dolly Campion, and all the other girls of her acquaintance, were there to see her.

They drove back in the same order. Then came dinner.

As Jenny took her seat at the table she perceived that a stranger was present, who sat on the right hand of Mrs. Lane, and to whom so much deference was paid that she guessed he must be somebody of note. He was dressed in a suit of black plush, slashed with yellow satin, and a black beaver hat; for gentlemen then always wore their hats at dinner. His manners charmed Jenny exceedingly. Whenever he spoke to either of the ladies, he always lifted his plumed hat for a moment. Even her model gentleman, Robin Featherstone, had never treated her with that courtesy.

Jenny was still further enchanted when she heard Mrs. Lane say to him, "My Lord."

So interested and excited was she that she actually presumed to ask Millicent, in a whisper, who the stranger was. Millicent only demolished her by a look. The steward, on the other side of Jenny, was more accommodating.

"That is my Lord Wilmot," he said; "an old friend of the Colonel."

Jenny would have liked to ask a dozen questions, but she did not dare. She already expected a scolding from Millicent, and received it before an hour was over.

"How dare you, Jane Lavender," demanded Jenny's superior officer, "let your voice be heard at the Colonel's table?"

"If you please, Mrs. Millicent," answered Jenny, who was rather frightened, "I think only Mr. Wright heard it."

"You think! Pray, what business have you to think? Mrs. Jane does not pay you for thinking, I'm sure."

Jenny was too much cowed to say what she thought—that Mrs. Jane did not pay her extra to hold her tongue. She only ventured on a timid suggestion that "they talked at the lower table."

"Don't quote the lower table to me, you vulgar girl! You deserve to be there, for your manners are not fit for the upper. Everybody knows the lower table is only for the household"—a word which then meant the servants—"but those who sit at the upper, and belong to the family, must hold their tongues. If we did not, strangers might take us for the gentlewomen."

Jenny silently and earnestly wished they would.

"Now then, go into the parlour and behave yourself!" was the concluding order from Millicent.

Poor Jenny escaped into the parlour, with a longing wish in her heart for the old farmhouse kitchen, where nobody thought of putting a lock upon her lips. She felt she was buying her dignities very dear.

What was she to do all this long Sunday afternoon? Being Sunday. of course she could not employ herself with needlework;

and though she was fond of music, and was a fairly good performer on the virginals, she did not dare to make a noise.

She was not much of a reader, and if she had been, there were no books within her reach but the Bible and a cookery book, on the former of which, for private reading, Jenny looked as a mere precursor of the undertaker.

Sunday afternoon and evening, at the farmhouse, were the chief times of the week for enjoyment. There were sure to be visitors, plenty of talk and music, and afterwards a dance: for only the Puritans regarded the Sabbath as anything but a day for amusement, after morning service was over. Farmer Lavender, though a sensible and respectable man in his way, was not a Puritan; and though his mother did not much like Sunday dancing, she had not set her face so determinately against it as to forbid it to the girls.

The long use of *The Book of Sports*, set forth by authority, and positively compelling such ways of spending the Sabbath evening, had blunted the perception of many well-meaning people. The idea was that people must amuse themselves, or they would spend their leisure time in plotting treason! and the rulers having been what we should call Ritualists, they considered that the holiness of the day ended when Divine service was over, and people were thenceforward entitled to do anything they liked. Yet there in the Bible was the Lord's command to "turn away from doing their pleasure on His holy day."

CHAPTER III.

The Gold that Glitters.

CHAPTER III.

THE GOLD THAT GLITTERS.

JENNY, crushed by Millicent, crept into a corner of the parlour, from which she amused herself in the only way she could find—watching the family and their guest, Lord Wilmot. They sat in the bay window, conversing in low tones, a few words now and then reaching Jenny in her corner, but only just enough to give her an idea that they were speaking of the young fugitive King, and of the sore straits to which he might be reduced. His stay at Boscobel House, and his subsequent adventure in the oak, so well known in future years, were discussed at length, for it was only a few days since they had happened.

"What a mercy the leaves were on the trees!" said Mrs. Lane.

"Ay, in very deed," replied the Colonel. "Had the boughs been bare, His Majesty had been taken without fail."

"I saw him two days gone," added Lord Wilmot, "and a sorry sight he was: his dress a leather doublet, with pewter buttons; a pair of old green breeches and a coat of the same; his own stockings, the embroidered tops cut off; a pair of old shoes, too small for him, cut and slashed to give ease to his feet; an old, grey, greasy hat, without lining, and a noggen shirt of the coarsest linen."

The word *noggen* originally meant made of hemp, and had come to signify any texture which was thick, rough, and clumsy.

"Poor young gentleman!" exclaimed Mrs. Lane.

"What a condition for the King of England!" said the Colonel, indignantly.

"Ay, truly," answered Lord Wilmot. "The disgrace is England's, not his own."

Mr. Lane was one of the party this evening.

He was an elderly man, and an invalid, mostly keeping to his own quiet room. Mrs. Lane, who was younger, and much more active, managed the house and estate with the help of her son; and the Colonel having for some years been practically the master, was generally spoken of as such among the tenants. The old man now rose, and said that he would go back to his own chamber. The Colonel gave his arm to his father to help him upstairs; and Mrs. Jane, turning from the window, caught sight of Jenny's tired, dull look.

"Come, we have had enough of talk!" said she. "Sweep the rushes aside, and let us end the evening with a dance."

"You were best to dance after supper," responded her mother, glancing at the clock. "There is but a half hour now."

Mrs. Jane assented to this, and going to the virginals, called Jenny to come and sing. The half-hour passed rapidly, until the sewer, or waiter, came to say that supper was served in the hall, and the party sat down.

As Jenny took her place, she saw Robin

Featherstone making room at the lower table for a stranger—a young man, aged about two or three and twenty, dressed in a tidy suit of grey cloth, and apparently a new servant. His complexion was unusually dark, and his hair jet black. He was not handsome, and as Jenny did not admire dark complexions, she mentally set him down as an uninteresting person—probably Lord Wilmot's man.

The good-natured steward, on her right hand, noticed Jenny's look at the new comer.

"That is Mrs. Jane's new man," said he kindly; "he goeth with you into Somerset. My Lord Wilmot hath spoken for him to the Colonel, and commends him highly, for a young man of exceeding good character."

Young men of good character were not attractive people to Jenny; a young man with good looks would have had much more chance of her regard.

"His name is William Jackson," added the steward.

Jenny was rather sorry to hear that this uninteresting youth would have to go with them to Bristol; the rather, because it destroyed the last vestige of a faint hope she had entertained, that Robin Featherstone might be chosen for that purpose.

The worst of all her grievances was, that she seemed completely cut off from his delightful society. She had really seen far more of him at the farm than she did now, when she was living in the same house. And then to have all her rose-coloured visions for the future destroyed—Jenny felt herself a badly used young woman.

Supper ended, the dance followed according to Mrs. Jane's decree, led off by herself and Lord Wilmot; and Jenny, to her great satisfaction, found herself the partner of the enchanting Robin.

"Mrs. Jenny, I have not had so much as a word with you since yestereven!" said that gentleman reproachfully.

"No, in very deed," assented Jenny; "and I hear you go not into Somerset, Mr. Featherstone."

"No such luck!" lamented the valet. I'm to be mewed up here. That black crow yonder will rob me of all your sweet smiles, my charmer."

"Indeed he won't!" said Jenny. "I don't like the look of him, I can tell you."

At that moment the new servant, and his partner, the dairy-maid, whisked round close beside them, and Jenny saw, from the amused twinkle in his dark eyes, that Jackson had overheard her disparaging remark.

"He looks as if he hadn't washed himself this week," observed Mr. Featherstone, whose complexion was fair.

"He's an ill-looking fellow," replied Jenny.

"Do you hear what they say of you?" asked Fortune, the dairy-maid, of her partner.

"I hear 'em," was Will Jackson's reply.

"Won't you knock him down?"

"I think not. Wouldn't be convenient to the Colonel."

"I doubt you're chicken-hearted," replied she.

"Think so?" said Will Jackson, quite calmly.

"Well, you're a queer fellow!" said Fortune.

"Hold you there!" was the reply; "I shall be queerer anon."

The Monday was a very busy day, for Mrs. Jane proposed to set forth with the lark on the Tuesday morning. She had obtained a pass from the Parliament for herself and friends, and four others were to accompany her; her cousin Mr. Lascelles, and his wife, and a neighbouring lady and gentleman named Petre. Jenny was very busy all day packing trunks and bags under the instructions of her young mistress. In the afternoon, as they were thus employed, Mrs. Lane came rather hastily into the room.

"Jane, child," she said to her daughter, "I am really concerned that you should have no better attendance in your journey than that fellow Jackson. I do indeed think we must send him back, and get you a more suitable man."

Mrs. Jane was on her knees, packing a little leather trunk. She looked up for a moment, and then resumed her work, giving all her attention to a troublesome box, which would not fit into the space that she had left for it.

"Is he unsuitable, madam? I pray you, how so?"

"Child, the man doth not know his business.

He is now in the yard, looking to your saddle and harness; and he doth not know how to take the collar off the horse. Dick bade him lift the collar off Bay Winchester, and he was for taking it off without turning it. And really, some of his——"

The sentence was never finished.

"O, Madam! O, Mrs. Jane!" cried Millicent, coming in with uplifted hands. "That horrid creature. I'm certain sure he's a Roundhead! Robin has heard him speak such dreadful words! Do, I beseech you, madam, tell the Colonel that he is cherishing a crocodile in his bosom. We shall all be murdered in our beds before night!"

Mrs. Jane sat back on the floor and laughed.

"Ah, my dear young gentlewoman, you may laugh," was the solemn comment of Millicent; "but I do assure you 'tis no laughing matter. If Mrs. Jane will not listen to reason, madam, I beg *you* to hear me when I tell you what I have heard."

The solemnity of Millicent's tones was something awful. Mrs. Jane, however, was so misguided as to laugh again; but her mother said, in a half-alarmed tone, "Well, Millicent, what is it? You speak of the new man, Jackson, I suppose?"

"Madam, Robin tells me that early this morning, as soon as my Lord Wilmot was gone, he went down to the blacksmith's with something of the Colonel's—a chain, I think he said, or was it——"

"Never mind what it was," said Mrs. Jane; "let us have the story."

"Well, he was in the blacksmith's shop, and to get out of the way of the blacks, which were flying all over, he had slipped behind the door; when who should come up but this Jackson, on Mrs. Jane's horse, that had cast a shoe. He could not see Robin, he being behind the door; I dare be bound if he had, he would not have been so free in his talk. You know, madam, what a horrid Roundhead the blacksmith is; Robin saith he wishes in his heart he never had to go near him. Well, as this fellow holds the horse's foot (and Robin says he did it the most awkward he ever saw), he asks the smith what news. 'Oh,' saith he, 'none that I know of, since the good news of the beating of the rogues of Scots.' 'What,' saith Jackson, 'are none of the English taken that were joined with the Scots?' Then, madam, the smith said, saving your presence, for really it makes me feel quite creepy to repeat such shocking words, 'I don't hear,' quoth he, 'that that rogue Charles Stuart is taken, but some of the others are.' Oh, madam, to speak so dreadfully of His Sacred Majesty!"

Mrs. Millicent's eyes went up till more white than iris was visible.

"Very shocking, truly," said Mrs. Lane. "Well, what further?"

"And then, madam, that Jackson said—Robin heard him!—'If that rogue were taken,' quoth he, 'he deserves to be hanged more than all the rest, for bringing in the Scots.' Oh, dear, dear! that I should live to tell you, madam, that a servant of my good master could let such words come out of his lips! Then quoth the smith, 'You speak like an honest man.' And so Jackson up on the horse and rode away."

"Well, it doth but confirm me in my view that the man is a most unsuitable guard for you, Jane. I shall speak to your brother about making a change."

"I don't think Jackson is a Roundhead," said Mrs. Jane quietly, rearranging some laces in a little box.

"Dear heart, Mrs. Jane! but what could the creature have said worse, if he had been Oliver Cromwell himself?"

"Well, and I do not think he is Oliver Cromwell either," replied Mrs. Jane, laughing. "And as to his not knowing his business, madam," she added, turning to her mother, "I pray you remember how exceeding good a character my Lord Wilmot gave him."

"My dear Jane! A good character is all very well, but I do want some capability in my servants as well as character. You do not choose your shoemaker because he is sober and steady, but because he makes good shoes."

"Under your correction, madam, he would not make good shoes long if he were neither steady nor sober. Howbeit, I pray you, speak to my brother: methinks you shall find him unready to discharge Jackson for no better reason than that he cannot take the collar off an horse."

"But the words, Mrs. Jane! Those awful words!"

"Very like they grew in Robin's brain," calmly answered Mrs. Jane, turning the lock of her trunk. "He is a bit jealous of Jackson, or I mistake."

"Jealous of that black creature!' cried Millicent. "Why, he could not hold a tallow candle to Robin!"

"I dare say he won't try," replied Mrs. Jane, with a little amusement in her voice.

Mrs. Lane, who had left the room, returned looking somewhat discomfited.

"No, I cannot win your brother to see it," she said, in rather a vexed tone. "He thinks so much, as you do, of the commendation my Lord Wilmot gave the young man. He saith he is sure he is not a Roundhead (I marvel how he knows); and as for his inaptitude, he said the man hath not been before in service, and hath all to learn. If that be so, it cannot be helped, and you will have to be patient with him, Jane."

"I will be as patient as I can, madam," said Mrs. Jane gravely.

"Oh, my dear Mrs. Jane! Oh, Madam! how you *can!*" exclaimed Millicent. "We shall all be murdered by morning, I feel certain of it! Oh, dear, dear!"

"Then you'd better make your will this evening," coolly observed Mrs. Jane. "Look here, Millicent, should you like these cherry ribbons? They would not go ill with your grey gown."

Millicent passed in a moment from the depths of despair to the heights of ecstasy.

"Oh, how good of you, Mrs. Jane! They are perfectly charming! I shall take the guarding off my grey gown to-morrow, and put them on."

"If you survive," said Mrs. Jane solemnly.

Millicent looked slightly disconcerted.

"Well, Mrs. Jane, I was going to tell you—but after what Madam said—if the young man be respectable—I don't know, really—this morning, as he was coming into the hall, I thought—I really thought he was going to offer to take me by the hand. It gave me such a turn!"

"I don't see why, if he had washed his hands," said Mrs. Jane.

"Oh, Mrs. Jane! what things you do say!"

Millicent had some excuse for her horror, since at that time shaking hands was a form of greeting only used between relatives or the most intimate friends. To give the hand to an inferior was the greatest possible favour.

"Well," said Mrs. Jane, locking the second trunk, "I expect Will Jackson is a decent fellow, and will attend me very well. At any rate, I mean to try him."

"Well, Mrs. Jane, I have warned you!"

"You have so, Millicent. And if Jackson murders me before I come home, I promise to agree with you. But I don't believe he will."

"Well!" repeated Millicent, "one thing is certain; the creature has surely never been in a *gentleman's* service before. I expect he has followed the plough all his life. But I do hope, Mrs. Jane, you may come back safe."

"Thank you, Millicent; so do I," answered Mrs. Jane.

The friends who were to accompany Mrs. Jane arrived at Bentley Hall on the Monday evening, and the party set out, eight in all, a little after five o'clock on the Tuesday morning. Mrs. Lascelles and Mrs. Petre rode behind their husbands; Mrs. Jane behind her new man, Jackson. For Jenny an escort was provided in the shape of Mr. Lascelles' servant, a sober-looking man of about forty years, whom she thought most uninteresting. So they rode away from Bentley Hall, Robin Featherstone kissing his hand to Jenny, and making her a very elaborate bow in the background.

The first day's journey brought them to the house of Mr. Norton, a relative of the Lanes.

"Remember, Jackson," said Mrs. Jane as she alighted, "I shall want my palfrey by six to-morrow morning at the latest."

Jackson touched his hat, and promised obedience. Mr. Norton led Mrs. Jane into the house, desiring his butler, whose name was Pope, to look to her man, and to put Jenny in the care of Mrs. Norton's maid. Jenny, being unused to ride much on horseback, was sadly tired by her day's journey, and very glad when bed-time came. She made one nap of her night's rest, and was not very readily roused when, before it was fully light, a tap came on Mrs. Jane's door.

Mrs. Jane sat up in bed, awake at once.

"Who is there? Come within," she said.

The answer was the entrance of Ellice, Mrs. Norton's maid.

"I crave pardon for disturbing you thus early, madam, but my mistress hath sent me to say your man is took very sick of an ague, and 't will not be possible for you to continue your journey to-day."

"How? Was ever anything so unfortunate!" cried Mrs. Jane. "Is he really very bad?"

"My master thinks, madam, he is not the least fit for a journey."

Mrs. Jane lay down again, with an exclamation of dismay.

"I do hope the young man is not weakly,"

she said. "'Tis most annoying. I reckoned, entirely, on continuing my journey to-day. Well, there is no help, I suppose, though this news is welcome but as water into a ship. We must make a virtue of necessity. Come, Jenny, we'll take another nap. May as well have what comfort we can."

And, turning round, Mrs. Jane went off to sleep again.

For three days Mr. Norton reported Jackson quite too poorly to ride; on the fourth he was a little better, and by the evening of the following Sunday it was thought Mrs. Jane might venture to resume her journey the next day.

They were up early the next morning, and as Jenny followed her mistress into the hall, Mrs. Norton being with them, Pope and Jackson came in from the opposite door. Jackson at once came forward to meet them, and for an instant Jenny was reminded of Millicent's complaint, for he seemed just on the point of shaking hands with the ladies. Suddenly he drew back, took off his hat, and with a low bow informed Mrs. Jane that he was ready to do her service.

The departure was fixed to take place after dinner; but before that meal was served, Mrs. Norton was seized with sudden and serious illness. Mrs. Jane showed great concern for her cousin, seeming to Jenny's eyes much more distressed than she had been for the previous postponement of her journey. While everything was in confusion, a cavalcade of visitors unexpectedly arrived, and made the confusion still greater. Mrs. Jane arranged to stay for some days longer, and act as hostess in Mrs. Norton's place.

As the party sat that night at supper, a traveller's horn sounded at the gate, and Pope, having gone to receive the new arrival, returned with a letter, which he gave to Mrs. Jane.

"Dear heart!" she exclaimed in surprise, "what have we now here? This is from my mother."

"Pray you open it quickly, cousin," replied Mr. Norton. "I trust it is no ill news."

"She was just tucking a bit of Southernwood into her bodice, when a voice . . . said softly, 'Jenny.'"

Mrs. Jane's reply was to bury her face in her handkerchief. She seemed scarcely able to speak; but Mr. Norton, to whom she passed the letter, informed the company that it contained very sad news from Bentley Hall. Mr. Lane had become so much worse during the week of his daughter's absence, that her mother desired her to return as soon as she had paid a hurried visit to her cousins in Somersetshire.

"I fear, cousin, we must not keep you with us longer," said Mr. Norton, kindly to Jane.

Mrs. Jane was understood to sob that she must go on the next morning. Too much overcome to remain, she left the hall, and went up to the chamber of Mrs. Norton, still with her handkerchief at her eyes. Jenny followed her, going into her bedroom, which was near to that of the hostess. She heard voices through the wall, accompanied by sounds which rather puzzled her. Was Mrs. Jane weeping? It sounded much more like laughing. But how could anyone expect so devoted a daughter to have the heart to laugh on this sad occasion?

When Mrs. Jane came out of her cousin's room, she was apparently calm and comforted. The handkerchief had disappeared; but considering the bitter sobs she had heard, Jenny wondered that her eyes were not redder.

The journey was resumed, and they arrived safely at Trent Hall, the residence of Colonel Wyndham, who was strolling about his grounds, and met them as they came up to the house. Mrs. Jane having alighted and shaken hands with her cousin the Colonel, it astonished Jenny to see Will Jackson go familiarly up as if to offer the same greeting. Remembering himself in an instant, he slunk back as he had done before, and took off his hat with a low bow. Colonel Wyndham, Jenny thought, looked rather offended at Jackson's bad manners, dismissing him by a nod, and calling one of his stable-men to see to him, while he took Mrs. Jane into the house. Jenny felt once again that Millicent must have guessed rightly, and that Jackson had never been in service in a gentleman's family before.

CHAPTER IV.

Sudden Changes.

CHAPTER IV.

SUDDEN CHANGES.

GREAT was the lamentation among the cousins at Trent House, when it was found that Mrs. Jane could stay only two days with them, instead of the two months upon which they had reckoned.

"I am the most to be pitied, Jane," said one of the young ladies, whose name was Juliana Coningsby, "for I start for Lyme in a week hence, and I had hoped to win you to accompany me thither. Now I know not what to do for a convoy."

"Well, I cannot go, Gillian," was the answer, "yet may I help you at this pinch. Take you my man as your guard; I can contrive without him, since my good cousin, Mr. Lascelles, is to return with me."

A little friendly altercation followed, Mrs. Juliana protesting that she could not dream of depriving her cousin of so needful a servant, and Mrs. Jane assuring her that the pleasure of helping her out of a difficulty was more than compensation for so slight an inconvenience; but in the end it was agreed that Jackson should proceed with Mrs. Juliana, returning to Bentley Hall when she should no longer require his services.

The party of eight, therefore, who had left Bentley, were reduced to four on their return, Mrs. Jane and Mr. Lascelles on one horse, Jenny and Mr. Lascelles' groom upon another.

They reached the Hall late on a Thursday evening, Mr. Lascelles suggesting when they came to the lodge that Mrs. Jane should sit and rest for a few minutes, while he rode up to the house to hear the latest news of Mr. Lane's health.

The woman who kept the lodge came out

courtesying to meet them, and Jenny wondered why they did not ask her how the old gentleman was.

Mr. Lascelles, however, had ridden hastily forward, and he soon returned with cheering news. Mr. Lane had "got well over this brunt," he said; and Mrs. Jane professed herself much cheered and comforted to hear it.

In the hall, as they entered, was Millicent.

"Well, Millicent, I'm not murdered, you see!" cried Mrs. Jane cheerily.

"Indeed, Mrs. Jane, I'm glad to see it, in especial considering all the warnings we've had. Three times of a night hath old Cupid bayed the moon; and a magpie lighted on the tree beside my window only this morning; and last night I heard the death-watch, as plain as plain could be!"

"Oh, then, that's for you, not me," responded Mrs. Jane quite cheerfully; "so look Jackson doth not murder you on his return, as he has left me unharmed."

Millicent looked horrified.

"Oh me! Mrs. Jane, is the fellow coming back?"

Mrs. Jane only laughed, and said, "Look out!"

Considering the chain of shocks and disappointments which Mrs. Jane had suffered, Jenny was astonished to see how extremely bright and mirthful she was, and still more surprised to perceive that this light-heartedness appeared to infect the Colonel. It was not, however, shared by Mrs. Lane.

"Well, Jane, child," she said one morning to her daughter, "I am truly glad to see thee so light of heart, in especial after all the troubles and discomfitures thou hast gone through. 'Tis a blessing to have a hopeful nature."

"Oh, I never trouble over past clouds when the sun shines again, madam," said Mrs. Jane cheerily.

"I marvel what we can make of your man, when he cometh back," resumed Mrs. Lane. "If you go not now again into Somerset, you will have no work for him to do."

"Maybe, Madam, he shall not return hither," answered her daughter.

"My cousin, Colonel Wyndham, had some notion he could find him a good place down yonder, and I thought you would judge it best to leave the matter to his discretion."

"Oh, very good," assented Mrs. Lane. "So much the better. I would not have the young man feel himself ill-used, when my Lord Wilmot spake so well of him."

"There is no fear of that, I hope," replied Mrs. Jane.

"O Mrs. Jane! I am so thankful to hear that creature may not come back, after all!" cried Millicent.

"Ay, Millicent, you may sleep at ease in your bed," said Mrs. Jane, looking amused. "But I marvel why you feared him thus. I found him a right decent fellow, I can assure you."

"Then I can assure you solemnly, madam," answered Millicent, with a look to match her words, "that is more than I did. Never can I forget the horrid moment when I thought that nasty black creature went about to take me by the hand. It made me feel creepy all over—faugh! I cannot find words to tell you!"

"Pray don't trouble yourself," calmly responded Mrs. Jane. "I am going upstairs, so you need not give yourself the labour to look for them."

Before many weeks were over, Colonel Lane came one evening into the drawing-room, to report a wonderful piece of good news.

"His Majesty hath escaped the realm!" cried he, "and is now clean over sea to France."

"God be praised!" exclaimed his mother. "This is indeed good news."

Farmer Lavender was almost as excited as his landlord, and declared that he would light a bonfire in the farm-yard, if he could be sure the stacks wouldn't get alight.

"Nay, Joe, I wouldn't," said his prudent mother. "Thou can be as glad as thou wilt, and the Parliament'll say nought to thee; but bonfires is bonfires, lad."

Will Jackson did not come back to Bentley,

and Mrs. Jane remarked in a satisfied tone that she supposed Colonel Wyndham had found a place to suit him.

Millicent contemptuously observed to Jenny that she wondered how Colonel Wyndham, who was a gentleman born, could take any trouble about that creature Jackson.

"Well, and I do too, a bit," said Jenny, "for I'm sure the Colonel did not seem over pleased when Will would have taken him by the hand as we was a-coming up to the house."

"No, you don't say!" ejaculated Millicent. "Did he really, now?—to the Colonel? Well, I'm sure, the world's getting turned upside down."

Millicent was considerably more of that opinion when a few months were over. Early one spring morning, before anyone was up, some slight but singular noises roused Mrs. Jane from sleep, and calling Jenny, she desired her to look out of the window and see what was the matter.

Jenny's shriek, when she did so, brought her

young mistress to the casement in a moment. Bentley Hall was surrounded by armed men—Parliamentary soldiers, standing still and stern—awaiting in complete silence the orders of their commander.

Mrs. Jane went very white, but her self-command did not desert her.

"Never mind screaming, Jenny," she said coolly. "That will do no good. They'll not take you, child; and these Roundheads, whatever else they are, are decent men that harm not women and children. I must say so much for them. Come quick, and dress me, and I will go down to them."

"Oh dear!" cried Jenny. "Madam, they'll kill you!"

"Not they!" said the young lady. "I'm not afraid,—not of a man, at any rate. I don't say I should have no fear of a ghost. Jenny, hast thou lost thy head? Here be two shoes—not a pair—thou hast given me; and what art thou holding out the pomade for? I don't wash in pomade."

Jenny, who was far more flurried and

frightened than her mistress, confusedly apologised as she exchanged the pomade for the soap.

"But—Oh dear! madam, will they take you?" she asked.

"Maybe not, child," said Mrs. Jane, quite coolly. "Very like not. I guess 't is rather my brother they want. We shall see all the sooner, Jenny, if thou makest no more blunders."

Jenny, however, contrived to make several more, for she was almost too excited and terrified to know what she was doing. She put on Mrs. Jane's skirt wrong side out, offered her the left sleeve of her kirtle for the right arm, and generally behaved like a girl who was frightened out of her wits.

Mrs. Jane, dressed at last, softly opened her door, and desired Jenny to follow.

"I will wake none else till I know what the matter is," she said.

"Come after me, and I will speak with the Captain of these men from the little window in the hall."

Jenny obeyed, feeling as if she were more dead than alive.

Mrs. Jane quietly unfastened the little window, and said to a soldier who had taken up his position close beside it—"I would speak with your Captain."

The Captain appeared in a moment.

"For what reason are you here?" asked the young lady.

"Madam, I hold a warrant to take the bodies of Thomas Lane, and John Lane his son, and I trust that none in this house shall impede me in the execution of my duty."

"My brother!—and my father!" exclaimed Mrs. Jane, under her breath.

"Sir, we shall not do that. But will you suffer me to say to you that my father is an old and infirm man, in weakly health, and I beg of you that you will be as merciful to his condition as your duty will allow."

The Roundhead captain bowed.

"Be assured, madam," he said respectfully, "that Mr. Lane shall fare better for the beseechment of so good a daughter, and that

I will do mine utmost to have him gently handled."

"I thank you, sir," replied Mrs. Jane, as she closed the window.

Then, Jenny still following, a little less frightened, since the enemy seemed after all to be a man, and not a very bad man either.

Mrs. Jane went upstairs and tapped at her brother's door.

"Who's there?" demanded the Colonel's voice very sleepily.

"The reward of your deeds," answered his sister, drily. "Make haste and busk thee, Jack; thou art wanted to go to prison."

"Very good!" responded the Colonel, to Jenny's astonishment. "Do you bear me company?"

"Nay; would I did, rather than our father."

"Our father! Is *he*——?"

"Ay. God have mercy on us!" said Mrs. Jane gravely.

"Amen!" came through the closed door.

"Jenny, go back to my chamber," said her

mistress. "I will come to thee anon. The hardest of my work lieth afore me yet."

For two hours all was haste and tumult in Bentley Hall. Then, when the soldiers had departed, carrying their prisoners with them, a hush almost like that of death fell upon the house.

Mrs. Lane had wept till she had no more tears to shed; her daughter did not weep, but she looked very white and sad.

"Now you mark my words!" said Millicent to Jenny; "'t is that Jackson has done it. He's played the traitor. Didn't I always say he was a Roundhead! Depend upon it, he's betrayed something the Colonel's done in His Majesty's service, and that's why that wicked Parliament's down on him. Robin, he says the same. He never did like that scheming black creature, and no more did I."

"Well, I don't know! He seemed a decent sort o' man, far as I could see, only that he wasn't well-favoured," said Jenny doubtfully.

"He was a snake in the grass!" said

Millicent solemnly; "and you'll find that out, Jenny Lavender."

To the surprise of the whole family, and themselves most of all, the prisoners were released after only four months' detention. That was considered an exceedingly short business in 1652. Neither father nor son seemed any worse for their trial; the Roundheads, they said, had not treated them ill, and had even allowed sundry extra comforts to old Mr. Lane.

So matters dropped back into their old train at Bentley Hall for about a month longer. Then, one August morning, Colonel Lane, who had ridden to Kidderminster, entered the parlour with an open letter in his hand. His face was grave almost to sternness, and when his sister saw it, an expression of alarm came into her eyes.

"A letter, Jane, from Penelope Wyndham," he said, giving her the letter.

"Mrs. Millicent and Mrs. Jenny, I pray you give us leave."

That was a civil way of saying, "Please to

leave the room," and of course it was at once obeyed. Evidently something of consequence was to be discussed.

"I do hope Mrs. Jane will not go away again," said Millicent.

"Well, I don't know; I shouldn't be sorry if she did," answered Jenny.

"Very like not; you think you'd go withal. But I can tell you it is vastly dull for us left behind. There's a bit of life when she is here."

Jenny went up to Mrs. Jane's room, where she occupied herself by tacking clean white ruffles into some of her mistress's gowns. She had not progressed far when that young lady came up, with a very disturbed face.

"Let those be," she said, seeing how Jenny was employed. "Jenny, child, I am grieved to tell thee, but thou must needs return to thine own home."

"Send me away!" gasped Jenny. "Oh, Mrs. Jane, madam, what have I done?"

"Nothing, child, nothing; 't is not that. I am going away myself."

"And mustn't I go with you?" asked Jenny, in a very disappointed tone.

"To France? We are going to France, child."

Jenny felt in a whirl of astonishment. Going abroad in those days was looked on as a very serious matter, not to be undertaken except for some important reason, and requiring a great deal of deliberation. And here was Mrs. Jane, after scarcely half-an-hour's reflection, announcing that she was going to start at once for France.

Mrs. Jane put her hand in her pocket.

"Here be thy wages, Jenny," she said. "Twelve pound by the year we agreed on, and thou hast been with me scarce a year; howbeit, twelve pound let it be. And for the ill-conveniency I put thee to, to send thee away thus suddenly, thou shalt have another pound, and my flowered tabby gown. Thou wilt soon win another place if thou list to tarry in service, and my mother hath promised to commend thee heartily to any gentlewoman that would have thee.

"So cheer up, child; there is no need for thee to fret."

Jenny felt as if she had considerable need to fret. Here were all her distinctions flying away from her at a minute's notice. Instead of being Mrs. Jenny, and sitting in the drawing-room at Bentley Hall, she would once more be plain Jenny Lavender in the farmhouse kitchen. It was true her freedom would return to her; but by this time she had become accustomed to the restraint, and did not mind it nearly so much. The tears overflowed and ran down.

"Come, come, child!" said Mrs. Jane, giving her a gentle pat on the shoulder; "take not on thus, prithee. Thy life is yet before thee. Cheer up and play the woman! Ah, Jenny, maid, 'tis well for thee thou art not so high up as some I could name, and therefore shalt fall the lighter. Now go, and pack up thy mails, and Robin shall take thee and them to the farm this evening."

"Must I go to-day, madam?" exclaimed Jenny, more dismayed than ever.

"I go myself to-day, Jenny," said Mrs. Jane,

gently but gravely. "The matter will brook no delay. Take thine heart to thee, and do as I bid thee: thou wert best be out of it all."

Poor Jenny went slowly up to the garret to fetch her bags, which had been stowed there out of the way.

As she came down with them in her hands, she met Millicent.

"You've had warning, have you?" said Millicent, in a whisper. "There's somewhat wrong, you take my word for it! You make haste and get away, and thank your stars you've a good home to go to. We're all to go, every soul save two—old Master's Diggory and me."

"What, Mr. Featherstone too?" exclaimed Jenny.

"Oh, he's going with the Colonel to France. But Master and Madam, they set forth tomorrow, and Diggory and I go with them. Mark my words, there's somewhat wrong! and if it goes much further, I shall just give my warning and be off. I've no notion of getting into trouble for other folks."

"But whatever is it all about?" said Jenny.

"Well, if you want my thoughts on it," whispered Millicent, in an important tone, "I believe it's all 'long of that Jackson. You thought he was a decent sort of fellow, you know. But you've to learn yet, Jenny Lavender, as all isn't gold as glitters."

"I think I'm finding that out, Mrs. Millicent," sighed Jenny; "didn't I think I was made for life no further back than yesterday? However, there's no time to waste."

She packed up her things, and made a hurried dinner; took leave of all in the house, not without tears; and then, mounting Bay Winchester behind Robin Featherstone, rode home in the cool of the evening.

"Farewell, sweetheart!" said Featherstone, gallantly kissing Jenny's fingers. "I go to France, but I leave my heart in Staffordshire, Pray you, sweet Mrs. Jenny, what shall I bring you for a fairing from the gay city of Paris? How soon we shall return the deer knows; but you will wait for your faithful Robin?" And

Mr. Featherstone laid his hand elegantly on his heart.

"Oh, you'll forget all about me when you are over there taking your pleasure," said Jenny, in a melancholy tone.

Mr. Featherstone was only half through a fervent asseveration to the effect that such a catastrophe was a complete impossibility, when Farmer Lavender came out.

"What, Jenny! come to look at us?" said he. "Thou'rt as welcome, my lass, as flowers in May. But how's this — bags and all? Thou'st never been turned away, child?"

"Not for nought ill, father," said Jenny, almost crying with conflicting feelings; "but Mrs. Jane, she's going to France, and all's that upset——" and Jenny sobbed too much to proceed.

Mr. Featherstone came to the rescue, and explained matters.

"Humph!" said the farmer; "that's it, is it? World's upset, pretty nigh, seems to me. Well, folks can't always help themselves — that's true enough. Howbeit, thou'rt welcome home, Jenny! there's always a place for thee here, if there's none anywhere else. You'll come in and take a snack, Mr. Featherstone?"

Mr. Featherstone declined with effusive thanks. He had not a moment to spare. He remounted Winchester, shook hands with the farmer, kissed his hand to Jenny, and rode away. And the question whether Jenny would wait for his return was left unanswered.

"I'm glad to see thee back, my lass," said old Mrs. Lavender. "Home's the best place for young lasses. Maybe, too, thou'lt be safer at the farm than at the Hall. The times be troublous; and if more mischief's like to overtake the Colonel, though I shall be sorry enough to see it, I shan't be sorry to know thou art out of it. Art thou glad to come back or not, my lass?"

"I don't know, Granny," said Jenny.

Kate laughed. "Have you had your fling and come down, Jenny?" she asked; "or haven't you had fling enough?—which is it?"

"I think it's a bit of both," said Jenny. "It's grand to be at the Hall, and ride in the coach, and sit in the pew at church, and that; but I used to get dreadful tired by times, it seemed so dull. There's a deal more fun here, and I'm freer like. But——"

Jenny left her "but" unfinished.

"Ay, there's a many buts, I shouldn't wonder," said Kate, laughing. "Well, Jenny, you've seen somewhat of high life, and you've got it to talk about."

Jenny felt very sad when she went to church on the following Sunday. The Hall pew was empty, and Jenny herself was once more a mere nobody in the corner of her father's seat. There was no coach to ride in; and very humiliated she felt when Dorothy Campion gave her a smart blow on the back as she went down the churchyard.

"Well, *Mrs.* Jenny! so you've come down from your pedestal? Going to be very grand, weren't you?—couldn't see your old acquaintances last Sunday! But hey, presto, all is changed, and my fine young madam come down to a farmhouse lass.

"How was it, Jenny? Did Mrs. Jane catch you at the mirror, trying on her sky-coloured gown? or had her necklace slipped into your pocket by accident? Come, tell us all about it."

"She gave me a gown, then," said Jenny, with spirit; "and that's more, I guess, than she ever did to you, Dolly Campion. And as for why I'm come home, it's neither here nor there. Mrs. Jane's a-going to France, to be one of the Queen's ladies, maybe, and that's why; so you can take your change out o' that."

Miss Campion immediately proceeded to take her change out of it.

"Dear heart, Jenny, and why ever didn't you go and be one of the Queen's ladies, too?"

"Oh, she's climbed up so high, queens isn't good enough company for her," suggested Abigail Walker, coming to Dolly's help.

"Mrs. Jane quietly unfastened the little window and said, . . . 'I would speak with you, Captain.'"

"Now, you two go your ways like tidy maids," said the voice of Tom Fenton behind them; "and don't make such a to-do of a Sabbath morning.

"Jenny, I'll see you home if you give me leave."

He spoke with a quiet dignity, which was not like the old Tom Fenton whom Jenny had known; and his manner was more that of a friend helping her to get rid of an annoyance, than that of a suitor who grasped at an opportunity of pleading his cause.

"I thank you, Tom, and I'll be glad of it," said the humbled and harassed Jenny.

So they went back together, Tom showing no sign that he heard Dorothy's derisive cry of—

"Room for Her Majesty's Grace's Highness and her servant the carpenter!"

The word lover, at that day, meant simply a person who loved you; where we say "lover," they said "servant."

At the farmhouse door Tom took his leave

"No, I thank you, Jenny," he said, when she asked him to come in; "I'm going on to Uncle Anthony's to dinner. Good morning."

And Jenny felt that some mysterious change in Tom had put a distance between him and her.

CHAPTER V.

Will Jackson Reappears.

CHAPTER V.

WILL JACKSON REAPPEARS.

FORTUNE MAY, the dairy-maid at Bentley Hall, came into the farm-house at supper-time that Sunday evening.

"Well, they're all gone," said she, "and the house shut up. They say the Parliament 'll send folks down to take it some day this week, and 'll give it to some of their own people."

"Ay, I hear Mr. Chadderton, whose land joins the Colonel's, has applied for it," answered Farmer Lavender. "Though he's a Roundhead, he's a friend of the Colonel's, and I shouldn't wonder if he give it him back when King Charles comes in."

"That'll not be so soon, I take it," observed his mother.

"The time's out of joint," said the farmer. "I'd as lief not say what'll be or won't be."

"Jenny, I've a good jest to tell you," said Fortune, with a twinkle in her eyes. "I did not see you in time afore you left the Hall. You'll mind, maybe, that Robin and me and Dolly Campion went together to the green, Sunday even?"

Yes, Jenny did remember, and had been rather put out that Featherstone should prefer Fortune's company to hers, though a little consoled by the reflection that it was on account of her superior dignity.

"Well!" said Fortune, telling her tale with evident glee, "as we went up the blind lane come a little lad running down as hard as ever he could run. 'What's ado? says I. 'Mad bull! mad bull!' quoth he. Dolly was a bit frighted, I think; I know I was. But will you believe it, Robin, he takes to his heels without another word, and leaves us two helpless maids a-standing there. Dolly and me, we got over the gate into the stubble-field, and hid behind the hedge; and presently we saw some'at a-coming down the lane, but I thought it came mortal slow for a mad bull. And when it got a bit nigh, lo and behold! it was Widow Goodwin's old dun cow, as had strayed. There she was coming down the lane as peaceable as could be, and staying by nows and thens to crop the grass by the roadside. We'd a good laugh at the mad bull, Dolly and me; and then says I to Dolly, 'Let's go and hunt out Robin.' So we turned back, but nought of him could we see till we came to the big bean-field, and then a voice comes through the hedge, 'Is he by, maids?' Eh, but he is a coward! Did you think he'd been so white-livered as that?"

Farmer Lavender laughed heartily. Jenny was exceedingly disgusted. She tried to persuade herself that Fortune's tale was over-coloured, perhaps spiteful. But one and another present chimed in with anecdotes of Featherstone's want of moral and physical courage, till disbelief became impossible.

"How will he get along in France, think you?" said Fortune. "They've naught but frogs to eat there, have they?"

On that point the company was divided, being all equally ignorant. But Farmer Lavender's good sense came to the rescue.

"Why," said he, "Jenny here tells me Colonel Wyndham's got a Frenchman to his cook; and he'd make a poor cook if he'd never dressed nought but frogs, I reckon."

"They'll have a bit o' bread to 'em, like as not," suggested the waggoner.

"Well, I must be going," said Fortune, rising. "Jenny, what's come of your grand gown as Mrs. Jane gave you? We looked to see you in it this Sunday. Folks 'll think it's all a make-up if you put it off so long."

"'Tisn't finished making up," said Kate, laughing.

"You'll see me in it next Sunday, if you choose to look," replied Jenny, in a rather affronted tone.

She was put out by Fortune's hint that the dress was considered a fiction; and she was thoroughly annoyed by the story about Featherstone's cowardly conduct. Bravery was one of the qualities that Jenny particularly admired; and she could not help feeling angry with Featherstone for thus lowering himself in her esteem. She thought of it many times during the week, when she was altering the flowered tabby to fit herself, and by the time that the dress was finished, Jenny's regard for Robin Featherstone was about finished also. Love she had never had for him; but he had flattered her vanity, and she liked it.

The next Sunday morning came, and Jenny dressed herself in the flowered tabby, with a pink bow on her muslin tippet. With a gratified sense of pride, she passed Fortune and Dolly Campion on her way up the churchyard; not less gratified to hear their respective whispers.

"Well, it wasn't a make-up, then!" said Dolly, in a rather disappointed tone.

"Dear heart! isn't she fine?" responded Fortune.

Little did Jenny Lavender think, as she

passed up the aisle to her father's pew, that the Jenny who entered that church was never to leave it again. There was a stranger in the pulpit that day—a man of a very different sort from the usual preacher. He was an old man, and the style of his sermon was old-fashioned. Instead of being a learned and closely-reasoned discourse, seasoned with scraps of Latin, or a political essay on the events of the day, it was a sermon such as had been more common in the beginning of the century —simple, almost conversational, striking, and full of Gospel truth. Such a sermon Jenny Lavender had never heard before.

The text was Gen. xxxii. 26: "I will not let Thee go, except Thou bless me." The preacher told his hearers in a plain fashion, without any learned disquisitions or flowery phrases, what blessing meant; that for God to bless a man was to give him, not what he wished, but what he really needed for his soul's welfare; that many things which men thought blessings, were really evils, and that all which did not help a man towards God, only hurried him faster on the road to perdition. He told them that Christ was God's greatest blessing, His unspeakable gift; and that he who received Him was in truth possessed of all things. When he came near the end of his sermon, he bent forward over the pulpit cushion, and spoke with affectionate earnestness to his hearers.

"Now, brethren, how many here this day," he said, "are ready to speak these words unto the Lord? How many of you earnestly desire His blessing? What, canst thou not get so far, poor soul? Be thine hands so weak that thou canst not hold Him? Be thy feet so feeble that thou canst not creep thus far up the ladder at the top whereof He standeth? Well, then, let us see if thou canst reach the step beneath—'Lord, I most earnestly desire Thy salvation.' Or is this too far for thy foot to stretch? Canst thou say but, 'Lord, I desire Thy salvation,' however feeble and faint thy desire be? Poor sinful soul, art thou so chained and weak, that thou canst not come even so far? Then see if thy trembling foot will not reach the lowest step of all: 'Lord, make me to desire Thy salvation.' Surely, howsoever sunk in the mire, and howsoever blind thou be, thou canst ask to be lifted forth, and to have sight given thee. Brethren, will ye not so do? When ye fall to your prayers this even, ere ye sleep, will ye not say so much as this? Yea, will ye not go further, and run up the ladder, and cry with a mighty voice, 'I will not let Thee go, except Thou bless me'?"

When Jenny Lavender came out of church, she stood on the second step of the ladder. She scarcely heard Abigail Walker's taunt of "Well, if Mrs. Jane did give her the gown, I'll go bail she stole that pink ribbon." Such things were far beneath one who had set foot on that ladder. And Jenny did not stay at the bottom; she ran up fast. By the time that she knelt down at her bedside for her evening prayers, she had come to the fourth step—"I will not let Thee go, except Thou bless me."

The last atom of Jenny's old admiration for

Robin Featherstone, which had been already shaken, vanished that day. The Spirit of God, who had touched her heart through the preacher, led her to see that folly, vanity, and frivolity were utterly out of concord with Him. And then came a feeling of regret for the unkind flippancy with which she had treated Tom Fenton. Jenny knew that Tom was a Christian man; it had been one reason why she despised him, so long as she was not herself a Christian woman. There was a gulf between them now, and of her own digging. Tom had given over coming to the farm except on business; he gave her a kindly "Good morrow!" when they met, but it was no more than he gave to Kate, or any other girl of his acquaintance; and Jenny saw nothing of him beyond that. On every side she heard his praises, as a doer of brave and kindly actions. She knew that, apart from the mere outside, there was not a man to be compared to Tom Fenton in the whole neighbourhood. It was bitter to reflect that the time had been when Tom was ready to put himself and all he had at her feet, and she had only her own folly to thank that it was over. No wonder Jenny grew graver, and looked older than she used to be. Her father was uneasy about her; he feared she was either ill or unhappy, and consulted his sensible old mother.

"Nay," said Mrs. Lavender, "Jenny's not took bad; and as for her sadness, it's just womanhood coming to her. Don't you spoil it, Joe. The furnace burns up the dross, and let it go! It won't hurt the good gold."

"You don't think then, mother, there's any fear of the dear lass going into a waste, like?" asked Farmer Lavender anxiously.

"No, Joe, I don't; I'll let you know when I do. At this present I think she's only coming to her senses a bit."

The old preacher appeared no more in the pulpit at Darlaston; but so far as Jenny Lavender was concerned, he had done the work for which he was sent there. Jenny had not a single Christian friend except old Persis Fenton; and she kept away from Tom's aunt, just because she was his aunt. She was therefore shut up to her Bible, which she read diligently; and perhaps she grew all the faster because she was watered direct from the Fountain-Head. Old Mrs. Lavender was wise in a moral sense, but not in a spiritual one, beyond having a general respect for religion, and a dislike to any thing irreverent or profane. Farmer Lavender shared this with her; but he looked on piety as a Sunday thing, too good to use every day. So Jenny stood alone in her own family.

While all this was passing at the farm, Colonel Lane and Mrs. Jane were speeding, post-haste, to France. The Colonel explained to Featherstone, whom alone of his servants he took with him, that he and his sister having had the honour of performing an important service to the King, their lives were in danger from the resentment of the Parliamentary party.

The King himself was now safe at Paris, where they hoped to join him; and on arriving there, if Featherstone wished to return home, he thought there was no doubt that he could get a passage for him in the suite of some person journeying to England. If, on the contrary, he preferred to remain in France, the Colonel would willingly retain his services.

"I have entered into arrangements," he concluded, "whereby my rents will be secure, and will be remitted to me from time to time while we remain in France. I trust it may not be long ere the King shall be restored, and we can go back with him."

Featherstone requested a little time to think the matter over. He certainly had no desire to leave the Colonel before reaching Paris, a city which he wished to see beyond all others.

"Ay, take your time," answered the Colonel. "My sister will provide herself with a woman when we arrive thither. In truth, it was not for her own sake, but for Jenny's, that she left her at home."

This conversation confirmed Featherstone in two opinions which he already entertained. First, he was satisfied that an understanding had been arrived at between the Colonel and his friend Mr. Chadderton, whereby the latter was to remit the Colonel's rents under colour of keeping the estates for himself. Secondly, he was more convinced than ever that Will Jackson had played the traitor, and that it was through him the Parliament had been made aware of the Colonel's service to the King's cause, whatever it might be.

Dover was reached in safety, and the party embarked on board the *Adventure* for Calais. It took them twenty hours to cross; and before ten of them were over, Robin Featherstone would have been thankful to be set down on the most uninhabited island in the Pacific Ocean, with no prospect of ever seeing Paris or anything else, might he but have been safe upon dry land. It was in a very limp, unstarched condition of mind and body that he landed on the Calais quay. Colonel Lane, an old traveller, and an excellent sailor, was rather disposed to make merry at poor Robin's expense; for toothache and sea-sickness are maladies for which a man rarely meets with much sympathy.

They slept the last night at St. Denis, where the Colonel encountered an old acquaintance, an English gentleman who was just starting for Paris, and who assured the Colonel that he should communicate the news of his approach to the King.

"Truly, I am weary of horse-riding as I may well be," said Mrs. Jane, as she mounted the next morning, to traverse the eight miles which lie between St. Denis and Paris. "Poor little Jenny Lavender! 't is well I brought her not withal; she would have been dog-weary ere we had won thus far."

For this short distance Mrs. Jane rode by herself, the Colonel mounting another horse beside her. Featherstone followed, and a French youth came last, conducting the baggage-horse. Rather more than half the distance to the capital had been traversed, when a large cavalcade was seen approaching. It consisted of a number of gentlemen on horseback, preceding one of the large cumbrous coaches then in common use, in which sat two ladies and a little girl. The coach was drawn by six heavy Flanders mares, which went at so leisurely a pace that they could easily be accompanied by a crowd of French sight-seers who ran before, behind, and all around them.

As soon as the two parties came within sight of each other, one of the gentlemen who preceded the coach rode forward and met the travellers, pulling off his hat as he came up to them. Featherstone perceived that he was Lord Wilmot.

"How do you, Colonel Lane?" he said. "Mrs. Jane, your most obedient! I pray you be in readiness for the high honour which awaits you. His Majesty comes himself to meet you, with the Princes his brothers, and the Queen in her coach, desiring to do you as much honour, and give you as good a welcome as possible."

"We are vastly beholden to their Majesties," replied Colonel Lane, looking as pleased as he felt, which was very much: for the honour thus paid to him was most unusual, and showed that the young King and his mother considered his service an important one. "Featherstone!" he called, looking back, "keep you close behind, or we may lose you."

Featherstone tried hard to obey, but found the order difficult of execution. The crowd was only bent on seeing the meeting, and cared not a straw whether Featherstone were lost or not. He knew not a word of French, and was aware that if he did lose his master, he would probably have no little trouble in finding him again. Moreover, he was very curious to see the King—partly on Kate Lavender's principle, of afterwards having it to talk about. Just at that awkward moment his horse took to curvetting, and he had enough to do to manage him. He was vaguely conscious that one of the riders, who sat on a fine black horse, had come forward beyond the rest, and was cordially shaking hands with Mrs. Jane and the Colonel. He heard this gentleman say, "Welcome, my life, my fair preserver!" and dimly fancied that the voice was familiar. Then, having reduced his horse to decent behaviour, he lifted up his eyes and saw—Will Jackson.

Will Jackson, and none other, though now clad in very different garb! He it was who sat that black barb so royally; the King's plumed hat was in his left hand, while the right held that of Mrs. Jane. It was at Will

Jackson's words of thanks that she was smiling with such delight; it was he before whom Colonel Lane bent bare-headed to his saddle-bow. The awkward lout who had never been in a gentleman's service, the ignorant clown, fresh from the plough-tail, the Roundhead, the traitor, had all vanished as if they had never been, and in their stead was King Charles the Second, smilingly complimenting the friends to whose care and caution he owed his safety. If the earth would have opened and swallowed him up, Featherstone thought he would have been thankful. But a worse ordeal was before him. As he sat on his now quiet horse, gazing open-mouthed and open-eyed, the King saw him, and the old twinkle, which Featherstone knew, came into the dark eyes.

"Ha! I see an old friend yonder," said he comically. "I pray you, fetch my fellow-servant up to speak with me."

Poor Featherstone was laid hold of, pulled off his horse, and pushed forward close to that of the King.

"How do, Robin?" asked the merry monarch,

who heartily enjoyed a little affair of this sort. "Nay, look not so scared, man—I am not about to cut off thine head."

Featherstone contrived to mumble out something in which "forgive" was the only word audible.

"Forgive thee! what for?" said King Charles. "For that thou knewest me not, and tookest me for a Roundhead? Why, man, it was just then the finest service thou couldst have done me. I have nought to forgive thee for save a glass of the best ale ever I drank, that thou drewest for me at breakfast on the morrow of my departing. Here, some of you"—His Majesty plunged both hands in turn into his pockets, and, as usual, found them empty. "What a plague is this money! Can none of you lend me a few louis?"

The pockets of the suite proved to be almost as bare as those of the King. The Duke of Hamilton managed to find a half-louis (which he well knew he should never see again); Queen Henrietta was applied to in her coach, but in vain, as she either had no money, or did not choose to produce it, well knowing her son's extravagance and thoughtlessness. Colonel Lane had a sovereign, which he furnished The King held them out to Featherstone.

"There!" he said, "keep somewhat for thyself, and give somewhat to the little dairy-maid that took my part, and would have had me knock thee down. Tell her she'll make a brave soldier for my Guards, when all the men are killed. Divide it as thou wilt. Nay, but I must have a token for pretty Mrs. Jenny." His Majesty cast his eyes about, and they fell on his plumed hat. Without a minute's consideration he loosened the diamond buckle. "Give her that," said he, "and tell her the King heartily agrees with her that Will Jackson's an ill-looking fellow."

It was just like King Charles to give away a diamond buckle, when neither he nor his suite had money to pay for necessaries. Robin Featherstone stepped back into the crowd, where he was pretty well hustled and pushed about before he regained his horse; but he managed to keep fast hold of the money and the diamond clasp. He was rather troubled what to do with them. The jewel had so pointedly been intended for Jenny, that he could scarcely help dealing rightly in that instance; but the division of the money was not so clear. A man who was just and generous would have given the 'sovereign to Fortune, and have kept the half-louis (worth about 8s. 6d.) for himself; but Featherstone was not generous, and not particularly anxious to be just. The portion to be appropriated to Fortune dwindled in his thoughts, until it reached half-a-crown, and there for very shame's sake it stayed.

"And why not?" demanded Mr. Featherstone of his conscience, when it made a feeble remonstrance. "Did not His Majesty say, 'Divide it as thou list'? Pray who am I, that I am not to obey His Majesty?"

Had His Majesty's order been a little less in accordance with his own inclinations, perhaps Mr. Featherstone would not have found it so incumbent on him to obey it. It is astonishing how easy a virtue becomes when it runs alongside a man's interest and choice.

Featherstone had never learned self-denial; and that is a virtue nearly as hard to exercise without practice as it would be to play a tune on a musical instrument which the player had never handled before. In that wonderful allegory, the *Holy War*—which is less read than its companion, the *Pilgrim's Progress*, but deserves it quite as much—Bunyan represents Self-Denial as a plain citizen of Mansoul, of whom Prince Immanuel made first a captain, and then a lord. But he would never have been selected for either honour, if he had not first done his unobtrusive duty as a quiet citizen. Self-denial and self-control are not commonly admired virtues just now. Yet he is a very poor man who has not these most valuable possessions.

Robin Featherstone stayed with the Colonel just as long as it suited himself, and until he had exhausted such pleasures as he could have in Paris without knowing a word of the French language, which he was too lazy to learn. What a vast amount of good, not to speak of pleasure, men lose by laziness! When this point was reached, Featherstone told the Colonel that he wished to return to England; and Colonel Lane, who, happily for himself, was not lazy, set things in train, and procured for Robert a passage to England in the service of a gentleman who was going home.

"I wonder how little Jenny's going on," said our idle friend to himself, as he drew near Bentley. "I might do worse than take little Jenny. I only hope she hasn't taken up with that clodhopper Fenton while I've been away, for want of a better. I almost think I'll have her. Dolly Campion's like to have more money, 't is true; but it isn't so much more, and she's got an ugly temper with it. I shouldn't like a wife with a temper—I've a bit too much myself; and two fires make it rather hot in a house. (Mr. Featherstone did not trouble himself to wonder how far Jenny, or any other woman, might like a husband with a temper.) Ay, I think I'll take Jenny—all things considered. I might look about me a bit first, though. There's no hurry.

CHAPTER VI.

Wherein Jenny makes her Last Mistake.

CHAPTER VI.

WHEREIN JENNY MAKES HER LAST MISTAKE.

"I MARVEL Tom and Jenny Lavender doesn't make it up," said Persis Fenton, as she laid the white cloth for supper on her little table. Here's Jenny got a fine sensible young woman, with God's grace in her heart (more than ever I looked for), and Tom goes on living in that cottage all by his self, and never so much as casts an eye towards her—and that fond of her as he'd used to be, afore, too! Tony, man, don't you think it's a bit queer?"

"I think," said old Anthony, looking up from his big Bible, which he was reading by the fireside, "I think, Persis, we'd best leave the Lord to govern His own world. He hasn't forgot that Tom's in it, I reckon, nor Jenny neither."

"Well, no—but one'd like to help a bit," said Persis, lifting off the pan to dish up her green pudding, which was made of suet and bread-crumbs, marigolds and spinach, eggs and spice.

"Folks as thinks they're helping sometimes hinders," replied Anthony, quietly taking off his great horn spectacles, and putting them away in the case.

"Tell you what, Tony, I hate to see anything wasted," resumed Persis, after grace had been said. "If there's only an end of thread over, I can't abear to cast it away; I wind it on an old bobbin, thinking it'll come in some time."

"The Lord never wastes nothing, wife," was Anthony's answer. "See how He grows plants in void places, and clothes the very ruins with greenery. It's always safe to trust Him with a man's life."

"Ay," half assented Persis, "but it do

seem a waste like of them young things' happiness."

"Where didst thou ever read in the Word, Persis, as happiness was the first thing for a man to look to? The Lord's glory comes first, and then usefulness to our fellows, a long way afore happiness. Bless the Lord, He do make it happy work for man to seek His glory — and that's what Tom doth. I'll trust the Lord to see to his happiness."

Just as the green puddings came out of the pan, Tom Fenton turned into the lane leading up to his own home, having been engaged in delivering a work-table that he had made for the Vicar's wife. It was a beautiful day at the end of October, very warm for the time of year, and the sun was near its setting. As Tom came to a turn in the lane, he saw a short distance before him, up a bye-road which led past Farmer Lavender's house, a solitary girlish figure, walking slowly, and now and then stopping to gather something from the bank.

A slight quickening of his steps, and a turn into the bye-road, soon brought him up with the solitary walker.

"Good even, Jenny!"

"Good even, Tom!"

For some seconds they walked abreast without any further speech. Then Tom said—

"I've just been up to parson's."

"Oh, have you?" replied Jenny, a little nervously.

"Their Dorcas saith she's heard as Featherstone's back."

"Is he so?" said Jenny, in a still more constrained tone.

"Didn't like it in France, from what she heard."

"Very like not," murmured Jenny.

"He's got a place with Mr. Chadderton—the young gentleman who was married of late, and who's coming to live at Bentley Hall; so you're like to see a bit of him again."

"I don't want to see him," said Jenny

suddenly. "I'd as lief he didn't come nigh me."

"You was used to like him middling well, wasn't you, Jenny?"

Before Jenny could answer, the very person of whom they were speaking appeared at a turn of the lane, coming towards them.

"Mrs. Jenny Lavender, as I live!" said he. "Now, this is luck! I was on my way to the farm——"

"With your back to it?" asked Tom.

Mr. Featherstone ignored both Tom and the question.

"Mrs. Jenny, since I had the delight of sunning myself in your fair eyes, I have had the high honour of beholding His Most Gracious Majesty King Charles, who was pleased to command me to deliver into your white hands a jewel which His Majesty detached from his own hat. He——"

"Me!" exclaimed Jenny, in so astounded a tone as to remind Featherstone that he was beginning his story at the wrong end.

"Oh, of course you know not," he said, a

little put out, for his speech had been carefully studied, though he had forgotten the peroration, "that His Majesty is Will Jackson. I mean, Will Jackson was His Majesty. At least——"

"Are you quite sure you know what you do mean, Mr. Featherstone?" demanded Tom. "Sounds as if you'd got a bit mixed up, like. Is it the King you've seen, or is't Will Jackson?"

Tom rather suspected that Featherstone was not quite sober. But he was, though between annoyance and self-exaltation he was behaving rather oddly.

"Look here!" he said angrily, holding out the diamond clasp. "Was Will Jackson like to give me such as this for Mrs. Jenny? I tell you, His Majesty the King gave it me with his own hand."

Suddenly Tom's conscience spoke. "Are you acting like a Christian man, Tom Fenton?" it said. "Have you any right to work Featherstone up into a passion, however foolish he may have been? Is that charitable? is it Christ-like?"

"Very good, Mr. Featherstone," said Tom quietly.

"I ask your pardon, and I'll relieve you of my company. Good night—Good night, Jenny."

Jenny could have cried with disappointment. She was afraid that Tom was vexed with her, and wholly unwilling to be left to the society of Featherstone. As to the diamond buckle, she did not half believe the story. Tom's action, however, had its effect upon Featherstone.

"Don't you believe me, Mrs. Jenny?" he said more gently. "I doubt I've made a mess of my story, but 'tis really true. Will Jackson was the King himself in disguise, and he bade me bring that to you, and tell you that he entirely agreed with you that Will was an ill-looking fellow."

When Jenny really understood the truth, she was overwhelmed. Was it possible that she had actually told King Charles to his face that she considered him ugly? Of course she was pleased with the gift in itself, and with his kindly pardon of her impertinence.

"But, eh dear!" she said, turning round the clasp, which flashed and glistened as it was moved, "such as this isn't fit for the likes of me!"

Farmer Lavender was exceedingly pleased to see the clasp and hear its story, and in his exultation gave Featherstone a general invitation to "turn in and see them whenever he'd a mind."

"Why, Jenny!" cried Kate, "you'll have to hand that down to your grandchildren!"

Jenny only smiled faintly as she went upstairs. She liked the clasp, and she liked the gracious feeling which had sent it; but what really occupied her more than either was a distressed fear that she had offended Tom Fenton. He never came to the farm now. The only hope she had of seeing him lay in an accidental meeting.

Sunday came, and Jenny dressed herself in the flowered tabby, tying her tippet this time with blue ribbons. When she came into the kitchen ready to go to church, her sister's eyes scanned her rather curiously.

"Why, Jenny, where's your clasp?"

"What clasp?" asked Jenny innocently. Her thoughts were elsewhere.

"What clasp!" repeated Kate, with a burst of laughter. "Why, the clasp King Charles sent you, for sure. Have you got so many diamond clasps you can't tell which it is?"

"Oh!—Why, Kate, I couldn't put it on."

"What for no? If a King sent me a diamond, I'd put it on, you take my word for it!—ay, and where it'd show too."

"I'd rather not," said Jenny in a low voice. "Not for church, anyhow."

"Going to save it for your wedding-day?"

Jenny felt very little inclined for jests; the rather since she was beginning to feel extremely doubtful if she would ever have any wedding-day at all. She felt instinctively that a jewel such as King Charles's clasp was not fit for her to wear. Tom would not like to see it, she well knew; he detested anything which looked like ostentation. And, perhaps, Christ would not like it too. Would it not interfere with the wearing of that other ornament of a meek and quiet spirit, with which He desired His handmaidens to adorn themselves? Jenny resolved that she would not put on the clasp.

"No, Kate, I shouldn't like to wear it," she said quietly. "I've got it put by safe, and you can see it whenever you have a mind: but it's best there."

"Thou'rt right, my lass," said old Mrs. Lavender.

"Well, I shouldn't like you to lose it, of course," admitted Kate.

Jenny fancied, and with a heavy heart, that Tom carefully avoided speaking to her in the churchyard. Old Anthony and Persis had a kind word for her, but though Tom went away in their company, carrying his aunt's books, he never came up to speak with Jenny. It distressed her the more because Kate said afterwards:

"Have you had words with Tom Fenton, Jenny? I asked him if he'd a grudge against you, that he never spoke."

"What did he say?" asked Jenny quickly.

"He didn't say neither yea nor nay," answered Kate, laughing.

The afternoon brought several young people, and there was, as usual, plenty of mirth and chatter. Jenny felt utterly out of tune for it, and slipped out of the back door into the lane. She went slowly up, feeling very low-spirited, and wondering what God was going to do with her. When she came to the gate of the bean-field—the place where Tom had overtaken her a few evenings before—she stopped, and resting her arms upon the gate, watched the sun sinking slowly to the west. Thinking herself quite alone, she said aloud, sorrowfully — "Oh dear! I wonder if I've never done anything but make mistakes all my life!"

"Ay, we made one the other night, didn't we?" said a voice behind her.

Jenny kept her start to herself.

"Yes, we did, Tom," she replied soberly.

"I've made a many afore now," said Tom gravely.

"Not so many as me," answered Jenny, sorrowfully.

"Tell me your biggest, Jenny, and you shall hear mine."

"There's no doubt of that, Tom. The biggest mistake ever I made was when I fancied God's service was all gloom and dismalness."

"Right you are, Jenny. That's about the biggest anybody can make. But what was the second, now?"

"Oh look, Tom, those lovely colours!" cried Jenny, suddenly seized with a fervent admiration for the sunset. "Them red streaks over the gold, and the purple away yonder—isn't it beautiful?"

"It is, indeed. But that second mistake, Jenny?"

"Nay, I was to hear your biggest, you know," said Jenny slily.

"Well, Jenny, the biggest mistake ever I made, next after that biggest of all that you spoke of just now—was to fancy that I could forget Jenny Lavender, my old love."

Two hours afterwards, the door of old Anthony's cottage opened about an inch.

"Uncle Anthony, are you there?"

"Ay, lad. Come in, Tom."

"Don't want to come in. I only want to tell you that the Lord's given me back the greatest thing I ever gave up for Him."

Old Anthony understood in a moment.

"Ay so, Tom? I'm fain for thee. And thou 'lt be glad all thy life long, my lad, that thou waited for the Lord to give it thee, and didn't snatch it like out of His hand. We're oft like children, that willn't wait till the fruit be ripe, but makes theirselves ill by eating it green. And when folks does that, there's no great pleasure in the eating, and a deal of pain at after."

"That's true. Well, good night, Uncle Anthony. I thought I'd just let you know."

"I'm right glad to know it, my dear lad. Good night, and God bless thee!"

It was not for nine years that the Lanes came back to Bentley Hall. Their lives would have been in danger had they done so at an earlier date. They came back with King Charles—when Oliver Cromwell was dead, and his son Richard had shown himself unfit to govern, and a season of general tumult and uncertainty had brought England into readiness to accept any firm hand upon the helm, and an inclination to look longingly to the son of her ancient Kings, as the one above all others given by God to govern her. But she had made the terrible mistake of first driving him away into lands where he found little morality and less religion, and it was to her woeful hurt that he came back.

It was on a beautiful June evening that the Lanes returned to Bentley: and the old master of the Hall only came back to die. Colonel Lane was looking much older, and his mother was now an infirm old woman. Mrs. Jane, a blooming matron of thirty, came with her husband, Sir Clement Fisher, of Packington Hall, Warwickshire, a great friend of her brother, and like him an exile for the King.

Charles did not forget the service done him by the Lanes, nor leave it unrewarded, as he did that of some of his best friends. He settled on Lady Fisher an annuity of a thousand pounds, with half that sum to her brother; and he presented Colonel Lane with his portrait, and a handsome watch (a valuable article at that time), which he desired might descend in the family, being enjoyed for life by each eldest daughter of the owner of Bentley Hall. They are still preserved by the Lane family.

A few days after the Lanes returned, Jenny Fenton stood washing and singing in the back yard of the cottage. Tom's work-shed ran along one side of it, and there he was carefully fitting the back of a chair to its seat, while a younger Tom, and a still more youthful Joe, were as diligently building a magnificent sailing-vessel in the corner. A woman of middle age came up to the door, lifted her hand as if to knock, stepped back, and seemed uncertain how to act. A child of six years old, at that moment, ran round the cottage, and looked up in surprise at the stranger standing before the door.

"Little maid, what is thy name?" said the stranger.

A little doubtful whether the stranger, who in her eyes was a very grand lady, was about to hear her say her catechism, the small child put her hands meekly together, and said—

"Molly, please."

"Molly what?" pursued the stranger, with a smile.

"Molly Fenton, please."

"That will do. Where's mother?"

"Please, she's a-washing at the back."

"Is that she that singeth?"

"Yes, that's her," returned Molly, carefully avoiding grammar.

The song came floating to them through the balmy June air.

> "'O God, my strength and fortitude,
> Of force I must love Thee!
> Thou art my castle and defence
> In my necessity.'"

The strange lady sighed, much to Molly's perplexity; then she rapped at the door. It was opened by Jenny, who stood with an inquiring look on her face, which asked the visitor plainly to say who she was.

"You don't know me, then, Jenny Lavender?"

"No, Ma—— Dear heart! is it Mrs. Millicent?"

"It is Millicent Danbury, Jenny. And I am Millicent Danbury still, though you are Jenny Fenton."

"Pray you, come within, Mrs. Millicent," said Jenny cordially. "I'm right glad to see you. There's been a many changes since we met—Molly, dust that chair, quick, and bring it up for the gentlewoman."

"Ay," said Millicent, with another sigh, as she sat down in the heavy Windsor chair which it required all Molly's strength to set for her; "there are many changes, Jenny, very many, since you and I lived together at Bentley Hall."

"Not for the worser, are they?" replied Jenny cheerfully.

"Ah! I'm not so sure of that, Jenny," answered Millicent.

"Well, I'm nowise afeard of changes," said Jenny, in the same bright tone. "The Lord means His people good by all the changes He sends. Mrs. Millicent, won't you tarry a while and sup your four-hours with us?"

The meal which our ancestors called "four hours" answered to our tea; but tea had not yet been introduced into England, though it was very soon to be so. They drank, therefore, either milk, or weak home-brewed ale.

"With all my heart," was the reply, "if I'm not in your way, Jenny. You are washing, I see."

"I've done for to-day, and Tom and me'll be as pleased as can be if you'll take a bit with us, Mrs. Millicent. Molly, child, fetch forth the table-cloth, and get the salt-cellar, and then run and tell father.—She's a handy little maid for her years," added Jenny, with motherly pride.

Millicent smiled rather sadly. "You are a happy woman, Jenny!" she said.

"Bless the Lord, so I am!" echoed Jenny. "It's the Lord's blessing makes folks happy."

"Say you so?—then maybe that is why I am not," said Millicent, rather bitterly. "I don't know much of the Lord."

"That's a trouble can be mended," said Jenny softly; "and you'll be main glad when it is, take my word for it."

"I don't know how to set about it, Jenny."

"Why, dear heart! how do you set about knowing anybody? Go and see 'em, don't you, and talk with 'em, and get 'em to do things for you? The good Lord always keeps His door open, and turns away none as come."

At that moment Tom came in, with a hearty welcome to his guest. Jenny, helped by Molly, bustled about, setting the table, and cutting bread and butter, while Tom drew the ale; and they had just sat down when a little rap came on the door.

"Anybody at home here?" asked a bright voice. Jenny knew it at once."

"O Mrs. Jane!—I crave pardon, my Lady! —pray you come in, and do us the honour to sit down in our house."

"I'll do you more honour than that," said Lady Fisher comically, as she came forward. "I'll eat that bread and butter, if you'll give it me, for I have been a great way afoot, and I am as hungry as a hunter."

"I pray you take a chair, madam, and do us so much pleasure," said smiling Jenny. "I have here in the oven a cake but just ready to come forth, made the Princess Elizabeth's way, His Majesty's sister, and I shall be proud if your ladyship will taste it."

"I'll taste it vastly, if I get the chance," said Lady Fisher, laughing, as Jenny took her cake out of the oven.

The Princess Elizabeth was that young gentle girl who had died a prisoner at Carisbrooke Castle, a few years after her father's murder, her cheek resting on the little Bible which had been his last gift. Her cake was a rich plum-cake, made with cream, eggs, and butter.

"Did you get your other honour, Jenny?" asked Lady Fisher, as she helped herself to the cake.

"Madam?" asked Jenny, in some doubt.

"Why, the jewel His Majesty sent you. I was something inclined to doubt Featherstone might forget it."

"Oh yes, madam, I thank you for asking, I have it quite safe. It was a vast surprise to me, and most kind and gracious of His Majesty."

"Well, now I think it was very ungracious in His Majesty," said Lady Fisher, laughing. "I am sure he ought to have sent it to Millicent here, who reckoned him a Roundhead and an assassin to boot, if he meant to show how forgiving he could be to his enemies."

"Oh!" cried Millicent, clasping her hands, shall I ever forget how the dear King took me by the hand? To think of having touched the hand of His Sacred Majesty——"

"Hold, Millicent! that's a new story," said Lady Fisher. "Last time I heard you tell it, that horrid creature, Will Jackson, only offered to take you by the hand. Has he got it done by now?"

Millicent looked slightly confused, but speedily recovered herself.

"O madam, I think he touched me. I do think I had the honour of touching His Gracious Majesty's little finger, I really do!"

"Really do, by all means, if it makes you happier; *I've* no objection. Jenny, I shall eat up all your cake. It is fit to be set before the Queen. Millicent, I wonder you can find in your heart to wash your hands."

"Oh, but I *had* washed them, madam, before I knew," answered Millicent regretfully.

"Well, I hope you had," answered Lady Fisher, "seeing there lay nine years betwixt. Heigh ho! time runs away, and we with it. Seems pity, doesn't it?"

"Depends on where we're running to," replied Tom, who had entered unseen. "Children that's running home, when they know their father's got a fine present for them, isn't commonly feared of getting there too soon."

"But how if folks don't know, Tom?" suggested Jenny, and Millicent's eyes reflected her query.

"My dear," answered Tom humbly, "it's not for the likes of me to speak afore such as her Ladyship. But I know what my dear old Uncle Anthony was wont to say: 'The only way to be certain you're on the way Home is to make sure that you are going to your Father; and to do that you must go with Him.' And I doubt if he'd speak different, now that he's got Home."

"Ay, I suppose we would all like to have God go with us," said Lady Fisher gravely.

"Madam, saving your presence, Uncle was used to say there's a many would like vastly well to have God go with them, that isn't half so ready to get up and go with God. David spake well when he said, 'Make *Thy* way plain before my face.' The Lord's way is the sure and safe way, and 'tis the only one that leads Home."

"I think, Jenny, you *are* a happy woman," said Lady Fisher, an hour later, as she took her leave. Tom had gone back to his work-shed. "Good night; God be with you."

"I am that, Madam, the Lord be praised,"

answered Jenny. "But the Lord is to be praised for it, for I've done nought all my life but make mistakes, until He took hold of me and put me right." *

* That part of the story which relates to King Charles and the Lane family is quite true, with the exception of a few small details. Authorities differ as to whether the King and Mrs. Jane rode to Trent House alone, or accompanied by the persons mentioned. Lord Wilmot followed them the whole time, at a safe distance.

www.ingramcontent.com/pod-product-compliance
Lightning Source LLC
Chambersburg PA
CBHW030337170426
43202CB00010B/1158